EDIBLE WILD PLANTS

OF

MARTHA'S VINEYARD

D0869640

By

Linsey Lee

Vineyard Conservation Society
P.O. Box 2189, Vineyard Haven, Massachusetts 02568

ACKNOWLEDGEMENTS

My thanks to everyone who helped and encouraged me in the preparation of this book; to my sister and brother-in-law, Kathleen and Dick Darman, whose support made the book possible; to Bob Woodruff, who took the time during the haying season to review the text; to all the people who contributed the recipes; to Mrs. White at the Scottish Bakehouse, who liked my pictures from the start and who never complained at the havoc "the Book" caused my working schedule; to George Mills, who took the time off from his own enterprises to proofread the text; to Pat and Isabel West, whose beautiful camp gave me the solitude and peace to write; and to my publisher, Katherine Tweed, who encouraged and bore with me at every turn.

For the 1999 reprint, thanks to: Carol Knapp, for her advice about plant populations; to Karen Huff, for her help with design and layout; and to the Vineyard Conservation Society, for reprinting the book.

This book is dedicated to the memory of my grandmother,
Helen Pratt Philbin.

First Printing 1975, Tashmoo Press
Second Printing 1999, Vineyard Conservation Society
© 1999 Linsey Lee

Library of Congress Catalogue No.
75 - 24889
Printed in the United States of America

This book should not be used as an identification guide.
The publishers and author cannot be held liable for any
problems resulting from using wild edible plants.

Book designed by Katherine Tweed
Printed by the Martha's Vineyard Printing Company

CONTENTS

Update to 1999 Edition

 Do not gather the following plants described in this book:

Fiddleheads - *Peteridium* and *Pteretis* species
Some members of these fern species are rare and it is difficult to distinguish in the fiddlehead stage of growth. Also, gathering fiddleheads can take one into fragile wetland areas, which should be avoided.

Indian Cucumber Root - *Medeola virginia*
Increasingly scarce on the Vineyard.

Jack-in-the-Pulpit - *Ariseama triphyllum*
Increasingly scarce on the Vineyard.

Mayapple - *Podophyllum peltatum*
Increasingly scarce on the Vineyard.

Milkweed - *Asclepias* species
Two members of the Milkweed family should not be gathered:
Wavy leafed milkweed - *Asclepias amplexicaulis*, is increasingly scarce. It has opposite leaves with wavy margins.
Although butterfly weed, *Asclepias tuberosa*, has recently been de-listed as a rare State species it should be appreciated in its natural setting and not disturbed. It is distinguished by its waxy leaves and orange flowers.

Shadbush - *Amelanchier* species
Nantucket Shadbush - *Amelanchier Nantucketensis* is a listed rare species occasionally found on the Island. It is hard to distinguish from the common shadbush, but is usually more bush-like and does not grow over eight feet high. So it is best to avoid collecting fruits from any shadbush tree or Juneberry bush under eight feet high.

Seaside Plaintain - *Plantago oliganthos*
Increasingly scarce on the Vineyard.

Wapatoo - *Sagitteria latifolia*
Increasingly scarce on the Vineyard.

4

FOREWORD

Since Wild Edible Plants was first published in 1975, the natural and human landscape of the Vineyard has changed greatly. Growth and development have fragmented natural environments. The locations described in the Introduction of this book as "open fields, less travelled roads, and quiet places in the woods" have all-too-frequently given way to house sites and new roads. Natural succession has also displaced plants adapted to open areas, as shrubs and trees invade the plains, old fields and bogs. The result is that many wild plants found in profusion twenty-five years ago are increasingly scarce.

The Island is still a beautiful place, but its plant habitats are strained. Indiscriminate gathering of the plants described in this book and the intrusion of people into some of the more fragile habitat areas will further disturb the delicate and tenuous balance between people and nature on the Island.

Wild Edible Plants has been reprinted in response to many requests, and I hope that it serves as a guide to the remarkable diversity and beauty of this unique place. The Vineyard's natural environment offers endless satisfaction and learning if we simply stop and take the time to observe. So enjoy the awareness of the wonder of the natural world around us that this book can help bring, but proceed with caution and respect in gathering.

Linsey Lee,
Tashmoo, 1999

INTRODUCTION

Long before Bartholomew Gosnold discovered Martha's Vineyard in 1602 the Island Indian inhabitants had been familiar with the useful and edible plants which grew wild on the Island, depending on them for food, shelter and medicine. When the first settlers arrived they were doubtless surprised to find to what extent the Indians had cultivated the Island's wilds. The Indians were careful not to overtax the Island's bounty by uncontrolled gathering of wild plants. They planted large fields of Jerusalem artichokes and cultivated many of the bogs where wild cranberries grew. Stands of fruitful hazelnut and oak trees were carefully tended, as were the areas in which the blueberries and blackberries were abundant. Certain special individuals were endowed with the knowledge of the preparation and locations of the medicinal herbs, and until recently there were a few older members of the Gay Head tribe who could still prescribe a concoction of wild Vineyard plants to cure almost any ill.

The early settlers soon realized that they too must live in close harmony with nature if they were to survive on this isolated island. Not that this was difficult; the Island waters teamed with fish, with little attention the land produced fruitful crops, and the fields and woods were filled with wild berries and greens which everyone gathered to supplement the garden produce. Being far removed from Boston and New Bedford, the Islanders learned to live in a state of almost total self-reliance. Until quite recently a trip off-island was arduous and time-consuming, and the people on the Vineyard continued to lead a life of cooperation with the land for perhaps longer than in most places in the United States.

A sense of isolation still exists on the Island, and most people who live and visit here still feel the desire to live in close contact with the land. The tradition of gathering food from the wild is still very much a part of Island life. To many Vineyard families expeditions for blueberries, blackberries and clams are an integral part of every summer, fall brings out the jelly makers to gather beach plums, elderberries and wild grapes to make fragrant preserves and wines. But most of the wild edible plants which are to be found on the Vineyard have been forgotten and ignored in these days of supermarkets and packaged foods. At this point most books would point out that all these wild foods are going to waste by the roadsides and exhort the reader to gather them. But before people rush out to scour the woods and fields, there are some important elements to be considered. Because the Vineyard is an island, the ecology of the land is extremely delicate and it has been made more so by recent building and development. It would be very easy to destroy total populations of many Vineyard plants by gathering them indiscriminately. If even a fraction of those who know about wild edible plants collected them on a regular basis the supply of some edible plants on the Vineyard would quickly be exhausted. Besides, hardly any of these plants are "going to waste". All of the plants, especially the flowering ones, play a vital part in making the Island the beautiful place that it is. What would the Island be like without fields of Queen Ann's lace and day lilies, hidden places in the woods where the violets and ferns grow, and dunes covered with wild roses, beach plum and beach peas? This book was not written to provide an alternative to grocery shopping on the Island nor as a survival handbook, but rather to point out another aspect of the bounty which the Island provides for us. Learning about which plants are edible and useful heightens our awareness of the land and vegetation around us. If you learn a little bit and your curiosity is aroused, the greenery of the roadsides and woods takes on whole new dimensions. The more you learn, the more you see, and the more you see, the more you learn. It sounds simplistic and obvious, but it is exciting. Searching for wild edible plants on the Vineyard takes you rambling into the fields, out to the beaches, along the less-travelled roads, and into the quiet parts of the woods. It is a peaceful and intimate way to get to know the Island well. The sense of the past, which always hovers so close on the Vineyard, is brought even closer when you learn to look at the land around you with some of the knowledge and objectives of our ancestors. You do not even need to eat wild plants to get all these benefits, but eating them is part of the fun. Almost all of the plants mentioned in this book really taste good if they are properly prepared, and some taste excellent. If you enjoy trying new foods, you will enjoy experimenting with wild edible plants; each one is a new taste experience, so do not expect them to taste like vegetables which you have tried before. Most wild greens tend to be extremely high in vitamins, and they have not been treated with dangerous chemicals and sprays. And, needless to say, they are free. So gather and enjoy wild edible plants, but do it with discretion and consideration.

One of the first and most obvious rules to follow when you gather wild edible plants is to be sure that you know what you are picking. Too often people get enthused about all this "food for free" and rush out gathering without properly preparing themselves with the exact identification of the edible and poisonous plants in their areas. The results in many cases have been disastrous. Poison hemlock may look just like Queen Ann's lace, or a deadly amanita like a meadow mushroom to an untrained eye, but mistaking the two could cost your life. The theory that you can eat whatever the birds and animals eat is not a reliable guide, as birds thrive on poisonous pokeweed berries and deer can eat mushrooms which would make a human sick. The only safe way is to become totally familiar with the appearance and probable location of any plant which you plan on eating. This means studying many different plant-identification books to get a really good idea of what each edible plant looks like. Studying the pictures in just one book can be misleading. Ideally when you first go gathering you should go with someone who is experienced in identifying wild edible plants in the field. Although most cases of misidentification result in nothing more severe than a stomach-ache, it just doesn't seem worth taking the chance.

As I have mentioned before, when gathering wild plants anywhere, especially on the Vineyard, use restraint. Gather only as much as you need to make a meal. Part of the advantage of wild edible plants is that they are so fresh. It is not a good idea to store the plants indefinitely unless you dry or freeze them. In any area where you gather, leave the majority of the plants undisturbed to assure repropagation. Do not gather from areas that may be polluted, such as well-travelled roadsides, sidewalks, or dirty streams.

I have made a few suggestions as to where certain plants may be found on the Island. This is just to give you an idea of locations the plants prefer; they are by no means the only places to find these plants. Remember that most of the land on the Vineyard is privately owned, and no one is going to appreciate your gathering Queen Ann's lace and day lilies from his front field. Ask permission before you go gathering on private land. Often locations will be noted as "waste places". This means any area of disturbed ground, such as vacant lots, roadsides or yards.

For each plant in the book I have discussed only the most basic ways of preparation for the table. When special treatment, such as prolonged drying or changing the cooking water frequently, is needed to make the plant palatable, I have noted this. Many of the plants are best prepared in the most basic way so you can taste their natural flavors. Many of the greens I have listed as "potherbs". This means they are to be treated like spinach, boiled or steamed for awhile and served with butter or vinegar or whatever appeals to you. You can experiment with any of the plants the same way you would with any store-bought vegetable; try milkweed buds in cheese sauce, fiddleheads sautéed in soy sauce, sorrel soufflé, or shadberry sauce on ice cream. At the end of the book I have included some recipes which show a few ways Islanders "fancy up" the wild plants they gather.

At first I planned to include only a few references to the medicinal uses of some of the edible plants. But I soon got caught up by the vital role the herbal cures played in the lives of people in the early days. The practice of herbal medicine was largely denounced as quackery in the beginning of this century with the advent of miracle drugs. Recently medical scientists have begun to realize that they may have spoken too soon. Recent chemical analysis of many of the plants used by Indians and "old wives" in treatment of diseases often prove that these plants contain significant amounts of the chemicals now manufactured artificially to treat the same ailments. Many medicines on the market today are still made from plant derivatives. Chokecherry bark, for instance, is still an important ingredient in many popular cough medicines. The essential oil of wintergreen leaves is still recognized by the U. S. Pharmacopoeia, the official listing of all scientifically recognized medicines, past and present, for its use as a painkiller and for flavoring medicines. More plant derivatives would certainly be in use if it were not for the fact that modern science finds it easier and more profitable to manufacture chemicals in the lab than to go out into the fields and woods to gather wild plants. Old herbals often seem laughable in their claims that certain plants will cure endless numbers of complaints from hysteria to loose gums. But often these long lists of miracle cures are not as ridiculous as they sound. In the early days before refrigeration and canning there were few sources of vitamins C and A available during the long winters, as they are most readily obtained from fresh fruits and vegetables. Severe deficiencies of these vitamins can cause such diverse and alarming ailments as depression, rotted gums, blindness, scurvy, and boils. So when the first humble greens appeared in the spring, loaded with vitamins C and A, they really were miracle drugs. Often one of the properties of certain plants is described as a "general tonic". These are usually the plants which are high in vitamins C and A and were taken in the form of a tonic or tea, or potherb, to act somewhat like a daily vitamin. Perhaps the most fascinating aspect of the practice of herbal medicine is the fact that many of the herbal cures were "faith cures"; the patient simply believed or was told that a certain plant would cure his ailment, and, in a surprising number of cases, these cures would seem to work, even though there is no medically proven reason why they did. One begins to realize that the dividing lines between fact and fantasy are not always as clearly defined as common sense would have you believe. Some plant medicines are extremely powerful and should not be used by anyone not well versed in herbal medicine. (And herbal cures should never replace one's doctor's advice in serious ailments.) But most are harmless to try and will be sure to have a beneficial effect.

For centuries man relied on the plant world for food and medicine, living harmoniously with nature much like any other animal. Progress and science have changed our status and outlook in the last century, and man now feels the natural world is at his service and under his control. On the Vineyard especially where the quality of life of a more peaceful era is still in the process of being radically altered by "progress," it is easy to see the critical turning point to which our arrogance has brought us. Learning about wild edible plants is not going to do anything to save the world or the Island, but it may open your eyes to the beauty and possibilities which exist in the natural world. If this book entertains and makes you see a few things of which you never were aware before, it will have served its purpose.

Linsey Lee
Lake Tashmoo 1975

Wild Grapes

WILD GRAPES - *Vitis species*

When Bartholomew Gosnold discovered Martha's Vineyard in 1602 he was impressed by the Island's beauty and the abundance of useful plants he found growing here, especially wild grapes and sassafras. He accordingly named the Island Martha's Vineyard after his daughter back home in England and the grapes which he saw growing in such profusion in every Island thicket and field. Long before he "discovered" the Island, the Indians had been familiar with the uses of the grape as a fresh fruit; or dried and mixed with other dried berries, such as shadbush berries and blueberries, to make their winter store of pemmican; as a dye plant, and as a medicinal plant. The early settlers also used the young leaves to stew meat in, in a way similar to Greek *dolmas*. Today Vineyarders still gather wild grapes in the fall to make into delicious jams, jellies and preserves. The Island wild grapes, mostly fox grapes, *Vitis labrusca,* are the ancestors of the cultivated Concord grapes and tend to be smaller and more tart than their domestic counterparts. In the past few years a number of people have decided to take advantage of the obviously ideal conditions for grape growing on the Island, and several vineyards of cultivated grapes have been planted. This year should find the first bottles of vintage Martha's Vineyard wine for sale in the stores, and hopefully these vineyards will become a viable Island industry.

Description Hardy, trailing vine bearing bunches of purple berries. Resembles domestic grape.

Location Open thickets, edge of wooded areas, fields.

Dates edible Leaves: June. Grapes: September - October.

Preparation Grapes: Jams, jellies, wine, preserves, etc. Leaves (gather when young but full-sized): Stuffed. (See recipes page 77).

Medicinal properties Wine: Induces sleep; promotes perspiration, relieves fever, "comforteth the heart and maketh glad the spirit." Leaves: Bound to head by Island Indians to relieve headache.

Uses Natural dye, deep purple.

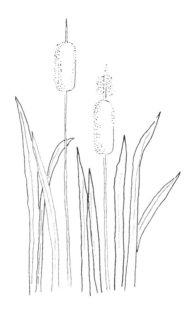

CATTAIL - *Typha latifolia*

Cattails grow in fresh or brackish water around the edges of swamps and ponds. On the Vineyard, cattails are found growing around most fresh-water ponds and also along the edges of salt-water bodies, such as Lake Tashmoo and Sengekontacket. As the cattail must have its roots in fresh water, this indicates that the fresh-water table surfaces at these points.

Description   3' - 8'. Leaves long, sword-like. Flowers in dense brown spike, commonly known as the "tail", on simple upright stalk.

Location   Edges of swamps and ponds.

Dates edible   All year.

Preparation   Inner white stalk of young shoots (gather in April to May until plant is about 2'): Raw, fried, boiled. "Tail" (gather in May to June when green and still enclosed by protective sheath): Cook and serve like corn on the cob. Pollen (covers "tail" soon after it breaks out of sheath): Use as flour; high in vitamin A. Central core of rootstalk (gather all year): Ground for flour. Dormant sprouts of next year's plant (bulb-like, found at end of rootstalks; gather September to May): Boiled, roasted, raw.

Uses   Down from tail: Stuffing for mattresses, lifejackets, pillows.

BEACH PLUM - *Prunus maritima*

The Cape and Islands are known nation-wide as the home of the beach plum. On the Vineyard, beach plum jelly-making is an art that has been perfected over the years - recipes are passed down from generation to generation and the locations of good beach plum picking places are closely guarded family secrets. However, you can find good recipes for beach plums in any Vineyard cookbook. Beach plum bushes flower before they bear their leaves and every branch is totally smothered with delicate white blossoms. In late May, the low-lying areas near the beaches where the beach plums grow look as if they were blanketed in fluffy white clouds, a very ethereal effect.

Description Spreading shrub, 3' - 6'. Branches black, bark rough. Leaves oval, shiny. Flowers white, 5 petals, resemble small apple blossoms. Fruit yellow to purple, approx. 1" in diameter, resembles small plum.

Location Poor, sandy soil near beach.

Dates edible Mid-August to September.

Preparation Plums: Jellies, jams, wine, juice, etc. (See recipe page 77).

Uses Plums: Natural dye, purples and reds.

Beach Plum

Cleavers

Indian Cucumber Root

CLEAVERS - *Galium aparine*

Cleavers is very common and quite pretty with its delicate white flowers, but it is so small and inconspicuous that most people never notice it. In the old days it was believed that eating quantities of boiled cleavers was a sure-fire method for losing weight.

Description Weak reclining plant that climbs over other vegetation. Stem thin, quadrangular, covered with clinging bristles. Leaves in whorls of 6 - 8 at intervals of 2″ - 3″ on the stem. Flowers small, white, star-shaped, borne on flower stalks at leaf whorls. Fruit small, round, bristly.

Location Moist ground, along stream banks.

Dates edible May - August.

Preparation Whole plant (gathered May to mid-June): Potherb, dried for tea. Fruit: Coffee substitute. To prepare, roast in slow oven and grind.

Medicinal properties Tea of dried plant: Relieves diarrhea, head colds; purifies blood; increases flow of urine; apply to face to remove sunburn and freckles.

 INDIAN CUCUMBER ROOT - *Medeola virginia*

The delicate Indian cucumber root is an easy plant to identify because of its distinctive leaf formation and flower. It is extremely tasty, having a distinct cucumber flavor and texture; however it should not be gathered indiscriminately, as digging the edible root destroys the whole plant, and it is not common on the Vineyard. Indian cucumber root grows best in moist, heavy woods, and most of the wooded areas on the Vineyard have quite light growth, as they were farm land within the last one hundred years. The only place that I have found it growing is at the Cedar Tree Neck Sanctuary where, of course, it cannot be picked. But it is sure to grow in other wooded places on the Island.

Description Single stemmed plant, 6″ - 12″. Leaves in whorls of 6 - 8 tapered leaves, two-thirds the way up stem, whorl of 3 - 4 leaves at top of stem. Flowers delicate, straw-colored, 3 recurved petals, 6 protruding stamens. Berries purple. Root tuber cucumber-shaped, 1″ - 2″.

Location Moist, medium to heavy woods.

Dates edible June to September.

Preparation Root tuber: Raw, boiled.

Uses Berries: Natural dye, purples.

15

CHICORY - *Cicorium intybus*

Chicory is an untidy, weedy-looking plant, but it has such bright blue blossoms that when it is in bloom it is a cheerful sight. The flowers tend to close when the sun becomes hot and are usually open only until noon. In mid-July the fields at Tashmoo Farm are covered with chicory in bloom and their white horses grazing against this carpet of brilliant blue make a delightful scene. In Europe and in the South, chicory is cultivated for its roots and young leaves. The roots make an inexpensive and caffeine-free coffee substitute which many people prefer to coffee. It is sometimes used alone but more often added to other coffee mixtures to enhance the flavor.

Description Randomly branched stalk growing from basal leaf rosette, 1' - 4'. Leaves basal, resemble dandelion leaves; on stalk, infrequent, sparingly toothed. Flowers bright blue, resemble flattened dandelion flower.

Location Sunny waste places, fields, roadsides.

Dates edible Leaves: April to mid-May. Roots: April to October.

Preparation Young leaves (cut off just above root): Raw in salads, potherb. Root: Dig, clean, slice, bake in slow oven 2 hours, grind and use like instant coffee. (See recipes p. 84).

Medicinal properties Root: Laxative; promotes perspiration; for jaundice. Flowers: Distilled into lotion used for eye inflammations.

Chicory

BEACH ROSE - *Rosa rugosa*

Nothing catches the essence of summer better than the smell of sun-warmed beach roses mingled with sea breezes on a hot day. In late summer on the Vineyard, beach rose bushes are laden with fruit, the orange rose hip, one of the highest natural sources of vitamin C. Most of the commercially sold vitamin C tablets are made from rose hips. Vineyarders for generations have realized the value of this fruit and have used it in tea, jams, and soup. It is hard to overestimate the importance of rose hips, as well as other fruits which could be dried or made into jams and pastes, to people in the days when no fresh source of vitamin C was available during the long winters. The rose flower itself is edible and it actually tastes just as it smells. The petals may be used as a base or flavoring, but the flavor is usually destroyed by long cooking.

Description Hardy, bushy plant, up to 5'. Branches covered with many thorns. Leaves oval, rough. Flowers deep pink, white, 6 petals. Hips orange, 1" - 2" in diameter.

Location Beaches, edge of dunes. Along road from Oak Bluffs to Edgartown.

Dates edible July to October.

Preparation Petals: Candied; flavoring; jams. Hips: Jams, jelly, soup, tea, stewed with meat. (See recipes pages 77, 78).

Medicinal properties Hips: Extremely rich source of vitamin C. Rosebud tea: Used by Apaches to cure gonorrhea.

18

BEACH PEA - *Lathyrus maritima*

Beach peas are a seaside variety of the Legume family, which includes garden peas and beans. The beach pea bears pods containing three to eight peas which are similar in appearance to garden peas and may be prepared in the same way. The dunes, especially those on the south side of the Island, rival any carefully tended flower garden when they are carpeted with the deep purple and pink blossoms of the beach pea in mid-July. With its long roots and spreading branches, the beach pea plays an important role in protecting the dunes from erosion by the wind and sea. Some sources claim that beach peas are poisonous, but many people have eaten them without ill effects. However, it is probably best to approach the beach pea with caution, eating only small amounts at first to see how your system reacts. All new wild edible foods should be approached with similar caution.

Description　Plant becomes reclining as it matures, spreads up to 3'. Stem stout, pale green. Leaves compound, 3-9 leaflets. Flower purple and pink, rarely white, pea-like. Pod resembles garden pea.

Location　Beaches, dunes.

Dates edible　July to August.

Preparation　Like garden peas. (See recipe page 79).

Beach Pea

Skunk Cabbage

SKUNK CABBAGE - *Symplocarpus feotidus*

Skunk cabbage seems to catch everybody's interest, perhaps because it is such a distinctive plant with its beautiful, fleshy, mottled purple and green flower and its heavy skunky smell, and because it grows in such profusion in damp Island woods and swamps before anything else is in bloom. People are always wondering if skunk cabbage is edible, but there is endless controversy on the matter, and most manuals tend to contradict each other over the proper way to prepare it for the table. Most sources claim that the first, still tightly folded, leaves to come up in the spring are delicious sliced and boiled in a few changes of water and a pinch of baking soda. Others, probably more experienced, say that the leaves and roots are edible only after prolonged drying of at least five months to remove the offensive odor and to destroy needle-like crystals of oxalate of lime which cause severe burning of the mouth and throat. All cases of so-called skunk cabbage poisoning can be traced to hellebore, *Veratrum viride,* which, although it has not yet been found on the Vineyard, grows in similar areas as the skunk cabbage and is often mistaken for it.

Description   Fleshy, mottled purple and green shell-shaped flower hood 3" - 4" with an inner, globular mass of lavender flowers. Leaves resemble small head of cabbage when first appear in spring, later unfold and are shaped like large elephant ear, 1' - 3'. Root 1' - 3'. Characteristic skunky odor.

Location   Swamps, moist woods, stream banks.

Dates edible   April.

Preparation   First leaves (still tightly folded): Sliced, dried for approx. 5 months then boiled, used in stews, etc. Roots: Inner core, sliced, dried for approx. 5 months; ground for flour.

Medicinal properties   Freshly dried root (listed in U. S. Pharmacopoeia 1820-1882, still listed in U. S. Dispensatory): Used for respiratory and nervous disorders; to cure rheumatism and dropsy; as an emetic, narcotic, antispasmodic, stimulant. Overdose causes vomiting, dizziness, dimness of vision. Potency diminishes with age. Root hairs: Applied to tooth cavities by Indians. Leaves: Burned and inhaled to cure headache by Micmac Indians.

IRISH MOSS - *Chondrus crispus*

Irish moss is a seaweed, found on all Island beaches, which acts like gelatin in making puddings and aspics. Until quite recently it was used in the manufacture of most commercially sold ice creams, and it is still in demand today as an emulsifier in chocolate syrups, as a base for many pottery glazes, and for use in hand lotions and cosmetics. The New England coastline produced the bulk of the commercially used Irish moss and after every storm people would rush to the beaches to rake it up. It has a high iodine content and imparts a subtle but pleasant flavor to any dish in which it is used. Most gelatine, being made from an animal base, is unacceptable to strict vegetarians, and so Irish moss is a helpful addition to any vegetarian diet.

Description Much branched, flattened, curly, pliable when wet, brittle when dry. Found in individual pieces or large mats. Bleaches from dark purple or green to pink or white as it is exposed to sun.

Location Beaches.

Dates edible Year around.

Preparation Used in puddings, aspics, ice cream, etc. Acts like gelatine when dissolved in hot liquid. (See recipe page 80).

Medicinal properties Soothing to digestive system; relieves diarrhea. Before World War II important source of iodine.

22

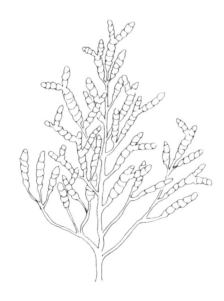

CHICKEN CLAWS, GLASSWORT - *Salicornia species*

This succulent, much jointed plant does actually resemble chicken claws except for its bright green color. The whole plant turns a bright crimson in the fall and forms striking carpets of color along the marshes and tidal ponds where it grows. The plant has a high soda content and was once used in the manufacture of glass and soap, hence the other common name of glasswort.

Description Small leafless succulent plant, 2″ - 6″. Resembles chicken claws or leafless pine tree. Stems cylindrical, conspicuously jointed, with small scales which are degenerate leaves. Bright green, turns red in fall.

Location Edges of marshes and salt water ponds. Lake Tashmoo. Poucha Pond.

Dates edible May to September.

Preparation Tender branch tips: Raw in salads, as garnish, potherb, pickled.

Elderberry

ELDERBERRY - *Sambucus canadensis*

Graceful elderberry bushes with their wide, drooping clusters of white flowers and dark purple berries are a common and beautiful sight along up-Island roads. The elderberry bush has been valued for its use in cooking, medicine and necromancy since ancient times. Islanders still gather the berries to make jams, jellies and wines high in vitamin C, but most people have forgotten that the elderberry flowers are also edible and delicious. However, there are a few things you should know before you go gathering from the elderberry bush. It was commonly known in the old days that witches often made their homes in elderberry trees. Therefore elder wood should never be burned in the home fireplace or made into a cradle. It is also necessary, when gathering the berries, flowers or branches of an elderberry tree, to ask permission of the resident witch. If this process is ignored, terrible misfortune will befall the gatherer. As protection against witches' curses, elderberry leaves were hung above doorways on Walpurgis Night, the witches' Sabbath on the last night in April. On the Vineyard, people often mistake viburnum for elderberry as it has similar clusters of purple berries. This is not a deadly mistake, but viburnum will certainly not make a very tasty elderberry jam and may cause a few stomach-aches. The main way to distinguish the two is to look at the leaves: the elderberry has pinnate leaves, a form of compound leaf, with five to eleven tapering leaflets, whereas the viburnum bears single, rounded leaves with jagged edges. The elderberry cluster is also large and drooping, the viburnum berry cluster stiff and flat. Fresh elderberries have a rank, "eldery" taste which most people find objectionable. When the berries are dried this flavor disappears. The dried berries are delicious stewed or in pies and can be used like blueberries in any recipe.

Description Slender woody shrub, 5' - 10'. Branches hollow. Leaves pinnate, 5-11 leaflets. Flowers cream colored, in large, spreading umbels. Berries dark purple, small, in drooping umbels.

Location Moist ground usually in vicinity of swamp or pond. Along Tea Lane, State Road in Gay Head, Middle Road.

Dates edible Mid-June to September.

Preparation Flower cluster: Fritters, added to cake mixes and pancakes, wine. Berries: Jelly, jam, wine, dried, in pies, etc. (See recipes page 79).

Medicinal properties Tea made from flowers: Induces perspiration; stimulant; increases flow of urine. Flowers mixed with cocoa butter and lanoline: Salve for burns; beautifies complexion. Berries (listed in U. S. Pharmacopoeia 1820-1831): General tonic; purgative; cough medicine; laxative. Inner bark: Emetic. Wine: Induces sleep, promotes perspiration. Leaves: Bury leaves on which three drops of blood from a wart are placed to make wart disappear.

Uses Berries: Excellent natural dye, purples and blue-grays.

25

SASSAFRAS - *Sassafras albidum*

Bartholomew Gosnold and his crew were on an expedition in search of sassafras when they discovered Martha's Vineyard in 1602. Gosnold was much impressed by the large stands of the tree he found here, and in the years that followed, ships from Europe and England would always stop at the Vineyard to pick up a supply of sassafras to take back to their home countries where it was highly regarded for its medicinal properties, especially as a cure for syphilis. In exchange, the Islanders would receive much needed finished products, such as tinware and tea, and so sassafras became the Vineyard's first marketable export. Sassafras has been called by another Latin name, *S. trifolium,* because each tree bears three differently shaped leaves: a simple entire leaf, a two-lobed leaf resembling a mitten, and a three-lobed leaf. Sassafras-root tea tastes delightfully like root beer and is worth drinking for enjoyment as well as for all its reputed medicinal values. Tea made from the twigs and leaves has a more spice-like, but equally pleasant flavor.

Description Slender tree, 5' - 30'. Trunk bark light brown, rough, branches green. Small trees can be identified in winter by green branches. Root has characteristic root beer odor. Leaves 3 types, as in illustration.

Location Wooded areas all over Island.

Dates edible Year around.

Preparation Roots: Tea, candy, flavoring. Dried leaves: Acts like gumbo file in soups, stews, etc. Leaves and twigs: Tea. (See recipe page 80).

Medicinal properties Roots: Spring tonic which clears blood of poison and rids body of excess weight, both accumulated through winter. Cure for syphilis; flavoring for medicines.

Uses Bark, leaves and twigs: Natural dye, tans. Twigs: Make good tooth brushes. Powdered bark: Good ant powder.

HAZELNUTS - *Corylus americana*

Hazelnuts are among the most prized and expensive nuts used in baking, but few people know that they grow wild all over the Vineyard. Squirrels and worms are extremely fond of these tasty nuts, so it is rare to find a fully matured bush of hazelnuts on the Vineyard with the nuts intact. In order to share in the bounty it is best to do your hazelnut gathering early in the season. Pick out a few good bushes in July and keep an eye on them all summer. Around late August the nuts are usually full-sized but still green, and this is the time to pick them, before the squirrels and worms get interested. Put them in a cupboard or closet for a few weeks to let them ripen. This method usually works, but you have to let the nuts get as ripe as possible before you pick them.

Description Woody bush up to 10'. Leaves egg-shaped, pointed tip. Nuts 1", enclosed in green sheath with distinctive ruffled edge.

Location Open thickets, meadows. Mostly up-Island. Often grows where high bush blueberry grows.

Dates edible Late August to September.

Preparation Nuts: Used like store-bought hazelnuts. (See recipe page 84).

DANDELION - *Taraxacum officinale*

Dandelion greens are probably the best known of all the wild edible plants. They are used as salad greens and as a potherb all over the world and are sold in many food stores in the cities, especially in Italian areas. In the days before frozen and canned vegetables, during the long winters people often suffered from a myriad of complaints ranging from blindness to scurvy caused by a severe deficiency of vitamins C and A, and so the gathering of the first spring greens which so miraculously cured all these ailments was a long anticipated event. Dandelion roots and greens are higher in vitamin C and A than most other greens, and the dandelion is always one of the earliest greens to appear, and so it gained great favor as a medicinal herb as well as a potherb. In suburban America people who do not know better regard the dandelion only as an unsightly blemish on their carefully manicured lawns and continue to spend money on vegetables which have been sprayed with chemicals and have a much lower vitamin content.

Description Familiar yellow-flowered plant with rosette of jagged-edged green leaves. Seedball fuzzy, white, globular.

Location Waste places, lawns.

Dates edible Late March to September.

Preparation Leaves (gather in early spring before plant flowers): Raw, in salads, potherb (may require change of water in cooking as plant matures). White inner crown of central rosette of leaves: Raw, potherb. Yellow mass of developing flower in center crown: Potherb. Root (until plant flowers): Boiled. To prepare, first peel and slice. Root (all season): Coffee substitute. To prepare, clean, slice, bake in slow oven until brittle, grind to a coarse powder. Flowers: Dandelion wine. (See recipes page 80).

Medicinal properties Tonic of leaves: Aids digestion; helps stomach complaints; used as cure for scurvy and jaundice; relieves anemia and purifies blood (because of high sodium content). Tonic of roots (listed in U. S. Pharmacopoeia 1831-1926): Laxative; relieves menstrual cramps.

Uses Blossoms: Natural dye, yellow.

Dandelion

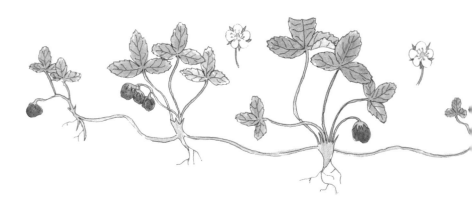

WILD STRAWBERRIES - *Fragaria virginiana*

Wild strawberries are usually a favorite of anyone who has taken the time to gather the small berries which are so much sweeter and more flavorful than any garden strawberry. It never seems possible to gather your fill of the berries, but perhaps this is for the best as it was commonly believed in Italy that strawberries could cause such a frenzy in children as to induce them to commit murder. The berry is not a berry in the proper botanical sense, *i.e.* the ripened ovary, but merely the enlarged receptacle or center of the flower. The name strawberry does not come from the practice of surrounding each plant with straw to protect the berries from rotting, but dates from older times when an obsolete form "straw" of the verb 'to strew' was used, referring to the way strawberry plants blanket an area in which they grow.

Description Familiar, resembles small garden strawberry, 1" - 4". Flowers white, 5 petals. Leaves in 3's, toothed margins, rounded tips.

Location Open sunny meadows.

Dates edible Mid-June to mid-July.

Preparation Berries: Fresh, jams, jelly, wine, etc. Leaves: Dried thoroughly for tea (wilted leaves are toxic). (See recipes page 81).

Medicinal properties Leaves: Relieves diarrhea; checks dysentery; astringent. Berry juice: Whitens teeth, relieves sunburn, whitens complexion.

GROUNDNUT - *Apios americana*

When the Pilgrims arrived in the New World it was too late in the season to plant crops, and they faced, among other things, the danger of starvation. Fortunately, some hospitable Indians showed them how to gather the edible tubers of the groundnut. These small, potato-like tubers were the mainstay of their diet for the first winters in the New World. Characteristically, within thirty years the grateful settlers had passed a law which imposed a heavy fine or imprisonment on any Indian found gathering groundnuts on "English land." Gathering the tubers can be tedious work, because the groundnut tends to grow in areas of dense vegetation, often mostly poison ivy, and following the root of a single plant can be difficult.

Description   Delicate trailing vine, climbs over other vegetation. Leaves pinnate, 3 - 7 leaflets. Flowers in clusters, reddish brown, cream colored keels, fragrant. Root a string of small round tubers, 1" in dia.

Location   Moist ground, along streams and ponds. Along Tea Lane.

Dates edible   Year around.

Preparation Root tubers: Raw, boiled, use like potatoes.

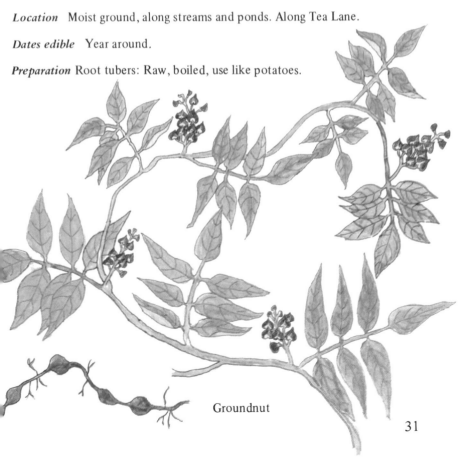

Groundnut

Pokeweed

POKEWEED - *Phytolacca americana*

Pokeweed can be a dangerous and troublesome weed, but it is also one of the best wild edible plants if it is gathered at the right time and prepared properly. In the spring and early summer the shoots of the young plants make an excellent potherb, but as the plant matures it becomes increasingly poisonous. Some books claim that the poison is contained only in the stem, berries and mature leaves, and that the new leaf tips are edible all season. But I would not want to take the chance, so I stay clear of the pokeweed once it has reached about six inches. Birds seem to find the attractive purple berries tasty and consume them without ill effect, but unfortunately the berries also entice children who eat them with more disastrous results, disproving the commonly held theory that "you can eat whatever the birds and animals eat." It is a plant you should learn to recognize both for its merits as a potherb and for the possible danger it poses to children and livestock. Pokeweed berries make an excellent and colorfast deep-red dye, with which you are familiar if birds who have been eating pokeberries have sat on your clothes line.

Description Large coarse plant, 2' - 8'. Stem thick, bright red. Leaves oval with tapering tips, large, alternate. Flowers greenish white, in drooping clusters. Berries purple-black, in heavy drooping clusters. Flowers and bears fruit until first frost.

Location Waste places, fields, roadsides. One of the first plants to grow in areas where the soil has been freshly turned over, such as along new dirt roads, in gardens, and houselots.

Dates edible May to June.

Preparation New shoots (gather before reaching 6"): Potherb. Boil in one change of water. (See recipe page 84).

Medicinal properties Dried root (listed in U. S. Pharmacopoeia 1820-1916): Relief of pain, inflammation, rheumatism, breast cancer; narcotic; purgative. Harmful in overdose.

Uses Berries: Natural dye, maroon.

YUCCA - *Yucca filamentosa*

This cactus-like plant is native to the Southwest and Spain and it grows in profusion in the deserts and plains of the western states, yet it seems quite happy here on the Vineyard. In Spain, rope and shampoo were manufactured from the tough fibrous root, and the Spanish settlers brought some of these useful plants with them when they came to the New World. The Vineyard yucca plants are probably descendants of these cultivated plants. Yucca was one of the staples of diet of the Indians in the Southwest. Yucca is a large, impressive plant with many fleshy white flowers, and when it is in bloom in July, it looks distinctly different from any other vegetation on the Vineyard. On the filled-in land on the Oak Bluffs side of the bridge near the hospital there are ten or twelve yucca plants which make quite a ghostly array in midsummer.

Description Leaves cactus-like, sword-shaped, with peeling tendrils, in rosettes, 1'-3'. Flowers cream colored, fleshy, bell-shaped, 2" - 3". Flower stalk solitary, leafless, branched, 3' - 8'. Seed pod peanut-shaped, mottled green, 2" - 4".

Location Dry, sunny, waste places. On Vineyard often used as ornamental lawn border.

Dates edible June to September.

Preparation Young flower stalk (gather in June before flowers form): Boiled, fried, roasted. To prepare, slice, remove skin after cooking. Young flowers: Raw, boiled, fried, roasted. Seed pods: Roasted, fried, boiled. Sliced inner pulp can be used like apples in cooking. (See recipe page 81).

34

STINGING NETTLE - *Urtica dioica*

One would not think that this infamous plant which causes such a painful sting when it comes in contact with the skin could ever be a palatable vegetable, yet people have eaten nettles for centuries, enjoying both their good taste and profiting from their unusually high vitamin and protein content. Nettles are even recognized by that bastion of food preparation, the Joy of Cooking, which lists a recipe for Cream of Nettle Soup. It is advisable to wear gloves while collecting nettles.

Description Plant downy, covered with stinging hairs, 1' - 6'. Leaves heart-shaped, jagged margins, alternate. Flowers small, green, in hanging clusters.

Location Waste places, farm yards, compost piles.

Dates edible May to June.

Preparation New shoots (gather until plant is 1'): Potherb. To prepare, wash in pot of water, stirring with long spoon, transfer shoots to cooking pot and cook in water still clinging to them for 20 minutes. (See recipe page 81).

Medicinal properties Potherb: High in vitamin C and A, relieves illness caused by deficiency of these; laxative.

Uses Woven into textile in Europe; excellent natural dye, greens; in Russia used to dye eggs yellow for Maundy Thursday.

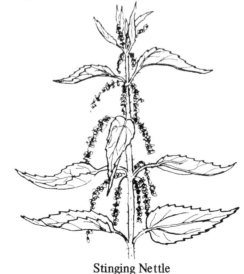

Stinging Nettle

BLUEBERRIES AND HUCKLEBERRIES
Vaccinium angustifolium, V. corymbosum etc.
and Gaylussacia frondosa

Every Vineyarder has spent countless hot summer days in the woods crouched among the blueberry bushes ("one for the bucket, two for me") or in the thickets up-Island in search of the more bountiful high-bush blueberries. Huckleberries tend to be blacker and rounder than blueberries, but for eating purposes there is no need to distinguish between the two. The Island Indians gathered great amounts of blueberries during the summers and ate them fresh, stewed them with meat and dried them for winter use.

Description   Ranges from small woody shrub to large bush. Leaves small, oval, slightly rough to touch. Flowers white to red, bell-shaped. Berries blue-black, round.

Location Wooded areas, sunny open thickets.

Dates edible August.

Preparation   Berries: Fresh, jams, jellies, pies, dried. (See recipe page 85).

Medicinal properties   Twigs and leaves: Contain active principle myrtillin, which lowers blood sugar; remedies abnormally functioning kidneys.

Uses Berries: Natural dye, purples and blues.

36

ACORNS - *Quericus species*

Oak trees are the most common trees on the Island and have long played an integral part in the lives of Islanders. Acorns were an important source of starch in the diet of Island Indians. The bark of the oak contains tannic acid and was used in tanning and dyeing. Oak is still used as fuel and for building. There are four kinds of oak on the Island, all of which bear edible acorns: White oak (*Quericus alba*), black oak (*Q. velutina*), post oak (*Q. stellata*), and scrub oak (*Q. ilicifolia*).

Description Tree, 10'- 40'. Bark rough, gray. Leaves lobed (see illustration).

Location All over Island.

Dates edible September to October.

Preparation Acorn: Whole, candied, in recipes calling for nuts, ground for flour. Before acorns are used they must be shelled and boiled in numerous changes of water for about 2 hours to remove the tannic acid and then dried in a slow oven for 1 hour.

Medicinal properties Inner bark (listed in U. S. Pharmacopoeia 1820-1916): Astringent; antiseptic; general tonic; cures diarrhea.

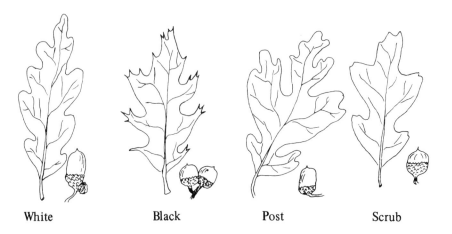

White   Black   Post   Scrub

Acorns

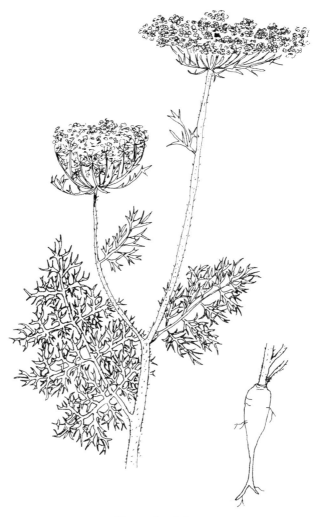

Queen Ann's Lace

QUEEN ANN'S LACE - *Daucus carota*

Queen Ann's lace is to me one of the most beautiful Vineyard wildflowers. A field of Queen Ann's lace, black-eyed Susans and bright yellow coreopsis swaying gently in the breeze is one of those Vineyard summer scenes that you store in your mind's eye to get you through the long, gray, winter months. Queen Ann's lace is also known as wild carrot because its roots smell and taste like carrots. It is in fact an escaped variety of garden carrot (or as some sources believe, the garden carrot is a cultivated form of Queen Ann's lace). You should be careful when gathering the roots, as poison hemlock looks somewhat like Queen Ann's lace and tends to grow in similar areas; mistaking the two could be disastrous. Before you go gathering, you should consult a flower-identification manual to acquaint yourself with the differences between the two. In the fall when the Queen Ann's lace goes to seed, the flower heads curl up to form what looks like a bird's nest (another common name for the plant), and at this point the seeds can be gathered for use as a seasoning much like celery seed.

Description Tall slender plant, 1' - 4'. Leaves feathery, much divided, resemble carrot leaves. Stems hairy. Flowers white, flat or slightly convex in lace-like cluster composed of bunches of many small flowers, often with a single, dark purple flower in center of cluster. Roots pale yellow, resemble carrot roots in shape and color.

Location Sunny, waste places, fields.

Dates edible Roots: June to September. Seeds: September to October.

Preparation Roots: Cook like carrot. Seeds: Used as seasoning. Be sure to winnow out fine hairs.

Medicinal properties Whole plant: Used in treatment of chronic kidney diseases and bladder infections. Seeds: Stimulant; expel gas from stomach; clear coughs, hiccoughs. Roots (listed in U.S. Pharmacopoeia 1820-1882): Encourage delayed menstruation; induce uterine contractions during childbirth.

Uses Whole plant (except root): Natural dye, yellows and grays.

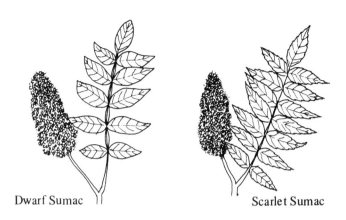

Dwarf Sumac   Scarlet Sumac

SUMAC - *Rhus glabra, Rhus copallina*

Abandoned farmyards and untended fields on the Vineyard soon become a jungle of sumac trees. These trees are hardy and fast spreading, but they have an almost tropical appearance with their graceful, feather-like leaves and clusters of red berries. They are one of the Vineyard's most colorful fall foliage trees, as their leaves turn from a bright orange to dark crimson. There are two species of sumac on the Vineyard: scarlet sumac (*Rhus glabra*) and dwarf sumac (*R. copallina*), both of which have edible berries. Though the two are similar in general appearance, their leaf structure is different. Many people are afraid of confusing edible sumac with poison sumac, but there is not much danger of this as long as you remember that poison sumac bears white berries in drooping clusters as opposed to the red, upright clusters of berries of the edible sumac.

Description Small tree, 6' - 12'. Branches covered with fine down. Leaves pinnate, 6-12 leaflets. Berries red, covered with fine hairs, in tight upright clusters.

Location Waste places, roadsides.

Dates edible August to September.

Preparation Berries: Sumac lemonade. Bruise berries in water, strain to remove fine hairs, sweeten to taste. One may also boil them for an excellent tea. (See recipe page 76).

Medicinal properties Roots: Tea of boiled root applied by Indians in western U. S. to open sores of gonorrhea; chewed to relieve mouth sores. Leaves: Applied as poultice to frostbite. Berries: Water in which berries have been boiled applied to stop bleeding after childbirth.

PURSLANE - *Portulaca oleracea*

Purslane grows rampant in almost every garden on the Vineyard. It is probably one of the weeds which you have always tried to get rid of, but now you should welcome it in your garden and pick it for your table along with the carrots and peas. Purslane is native to India and grows in all tropical countries. It is a succulent plant and its mucilaginous qualities make it a good plant to add to soups and stews to thicken the consistency as well as liven up the flavor.

Description Succulent, ground-hugging plant, approx. 3″ high, spreads up to 3′ across. Stems rounded, reddish, much forked, grow radiating from central stem. Leaves blunt-tipped. Flowers small, yellow, borne at forks between leaves, open only on sunny mornings. Seed pods small, boxlike, contain many tiny black seeds.

Location Gardens, waste places.

Dates edible May to August.

Preparation New leaves: Raw, potherb, added to soups and stews. Stems: Pickled. Seeds: Ground for flour. (See recipes pages 81, 84).

Medicinal properties Whole plant boiled with honey: Relieves coughs.

Uses Natural dye, tans and browns.

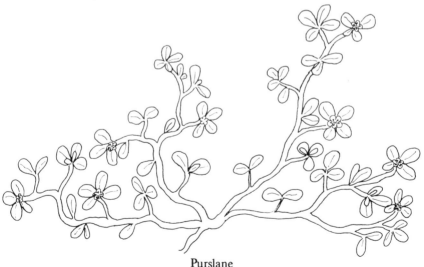

Purslane

41

SEASIDE PLANTAIN - *Plantago oliganthos*

Seaside plantain is closely related to the common plantain, the unsightly weed of lawns and gardens. It is similar in appearance to the common plantain, except that it has succulent grass-like leaves which earn it the other common name of goose tongue.

Description 4" - 8". Leaves thin, grass-like, succulent, gray-green, grow in rosette. Flowers minute, drab green, borne on slender central stalk, resemble common plantain flowers.

Location Edge of salt water ponds. Along Sengekontacket at Felix Neck. Around salt water marshes behind dunes in Wasque.

Dates edible June to August.

Preparation Leaves: Raw, potherb.

PIGWEED OR LAMB'S-QUARTERS - *Chenopodium album*

Pigweed or lamb's-quarters grows in almost every garden and vacant lot of the Vineyard. It is similar in appearance to and as variable as the beach-growing orach. And, like orach, it is closely related to spinach.

Description Extremely variable. Resembles orach, page 47.

Location Gardens, waste places.

Dates edible Leaves: June to August. Seeds: October.

Preparation New leaves: Raw, potherb. Seeds: Ground for flour. (See recipes pages 81, 84).

WATERCRESS - *Nasturtium officinale*

Watercress, just like the kind you buy in the store, grows free for the picking all over the Island. It grows in the shallows of running streams and can be gathered from early spring into the fall. Be careful not to gather watercress from polluted water.

Description Identical with store-bought watercress.

Location Running streams, ponds. Head of the Lagoon.

Dates edible April to September.

Preparation Use like store-bought watercress. (See recipes page 84).

42

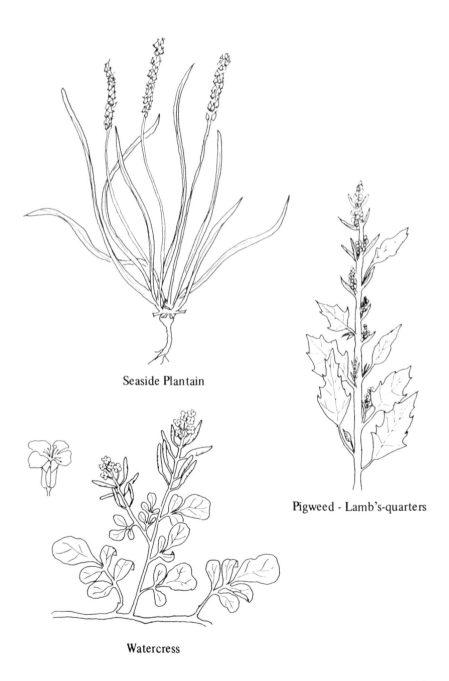

Seaside Plantain

Pigweed - Lamb's-quarters

Watercress

43

Sorrel

Mustard

SORREL - *Rumex acetosella*

This inconspicuous plant is one of the more versatile, wild edible plants. Its leaves have a lemony flavor and can be used in both vegetable dishes and desserts. In Europe it is raised as a garden vegetable, but here it is regarded as a troublesome weed which invades gardens and lawns. When it blooms it covers the ground with a luxurious carpet of rusty red, one of the first bright colors of the subtle Vineyard spring.

Description 2" - 8". Leaves arrow-shaped. Flowers red or green, bell-shaped, borne on central flower stalk.

Location Waste places, prefers acid soil.

Dates edible April to September.

Preparation New leaves: Raw in salads, garnish, sandwiches, potherb, soup, use like rhubarb in desserts. (See recipes pages 82, 84).

Medicinal properties Sharpens appetite; cools blood; cures scurvy.

MUSTARD - *Brassica species*

There are many members of the Mustard family growing on the Vineyard and a great number of them are edible. Discussed here is a typical member of the family, the Brassica species. Other edible species which I have listed below are more or less similar in appearance and can be gathered and prepared in similar ways. Any flower guide will show you what they look like. Mustard is one of the earliest spring greens and it is packed with vitamins A, B, B1, and C. It grows almost anywhere and most people regard it as a bothersome weed, but I have seen it planted in some Vineyard gardens, alongside domestic members of the Mustard family: broccoli, radishes, cauliflowers and Brussels sprouts. Once it blooms, the time to pick the edible greens is past, but it is still enjoyable as one of the earliest and most colorful spring flowers.

Description Weedy looking plant, 8" - 3'. Leaves lyre-shaped, irregular margins, mostly basal. Flowers yellow, 4 petals, 6 stamens. Pods narrow, 4 sided, 1" - 2".

Location Waste places, gardens, fields.

Dates edible Late April to June.

Preparation First leaves in spring: Potherb, raw in salads. Flower buds: Cook like broccoli. Seeds: Dried and ground for mustard. (See recipes page 84).

Medicinal properties Seeds in boiling water: Emetic; inducing vomiting. Seeds made into plaster: Relieves aches and fever.

Other edible Mustards Poorman's Peppergrass - *Lepidum virginicum.* Shepherd's Purse - *Capsella bursa-pastoris* Wintercress - *Barbarea vulgaris.* Wild radish - *Raphanus raphanistrum.*

45

 MILKWEED - *Asclepias syriaca*

Everyone is familiar with milkweed, the coarse, common weed of farmyard and fields, but few people are aware of how many edible dishes this weed produces. There are many members of the Milkweed family on the Vineyard, including the beautiful, bright orange, butterfly weed, the favorite haunt of the Monarch butterfly, and the colorful, purple, swamp milkweed. The common milkweed, *Asclepias syriaca,* is the one usually gathered for eating as it is so abundant and grows in easily accessible places. Some scholars believe that the sacred Soma of Hindu mythology was a personification of a species of milkweed plant, and that the intoxicating ceremonial potion was prepared from the plant's milky juice.

Description Large, coarse plant, 1' - 5'. Stem thick, generally unbranched, exudes milky juice when broken. Leaves oval, blunt. Flowers greenish white to purple, star-shaped, tubular, in clusters. Pods 2" - 4", containing many brown seeds with white feathery "parachutes".

Location Waste places, fields.

Dates edible May to August.

Preparation New shoots (gather when first appear in spring until 6"): Serve like asparagus. Unopened flower buds: Serve like broccoli. Young pods (1" -2"): Serve like okra. Milkweed contains a bitter principle that must be removed by cooking each milkweed product in three or four changes of water. For example, to cook milkweed pods, add pods to boiling water, cook for one minute, drain, and add boiling water. Repeat this process several times. Then cook in the last change of water for about ten minutes.

Medicinal properties Infusion of pounded root: Drunk by Indians to insure temporary sterility; relieves kidney complaints. Milky juice from stem: Cures ring worm; used to remove warts by Indians.

Uses Root: Made into fiber in France and Russia. Stems: Made into brooms used for sweeping rooms infested with fleas.

ORACH - *Atriplex species*

Orach is a beach-growing plant that is closely related to spinach. It has the same high vitamin content as spinach plus extra minerals that it receives from constant exposure to the mineral-laden salt sea air. It often grows upright, to a height of three feet, resembling a well proportioned tree, but it can also be a single unbranched stem which sprawls untidily on the beach.

Description   Extremely variable, 6" - 4'. Stem gray-green to red, upright or reclining. Leaves arrow-shaped, mealy, dark green above, light green below.

Location Beach above high water mark. Mostly on north side of Island.

Dates edible   June to September.

Preparation New leaves: Raw, potherb. (See recipe page 84).

Medicinal properties   Whole plant: Relieves hysteria.

Orach

CHOKECHERRY - *Prunus virginiana, Prunus serotina*

Chokecherries and wild cherries are among the wild fruits that go unappreciated by most Vineyarders except the birds. Although most chokecherries are too tart to be enjoyed right off the tree, they make delicious jams and jellies. The cherries are easily picked by hand off the smaller bushes; when gathering from the larger trees, spread out a sheet below the tree and shake the fruit down.

Description Bush or tree, 5' - 50'. Easily identified in winter by scaly blight on branches. Trunk bark rough, black. Branches smooth grey, or reddish. Leaves oval, shiny. Flowers white, borne in hanging spikes. Fruit dark purple, borne in hanging spikes.

Location Open places, woods.

Dates edible August to September.

Preparation Fruit: Jams, jellies, wine. (See recipe page 82).

Medicinal properties Inner bark (listed in U. S. Pharmacopoeia since 1820): Important ingredient in cough syrups, has sedative effect on nerves of respiratory system.

Uses Bark: Natural dye, reddish brown. Fruit: Natural dye, reds.

48

 SHADBUSH BERRIES and JUNEBERRIES
Amelanchier species

In mid-May when the Island woods are just beginning to stir with life - the branches of the oak trees are turning red with new sap and the trees along the roadsides have unfolded the smallest gold-green leaves - the shadbush trees come into full bloom. Their slender branches covered with drooping clusters of delicate white flowers, they fill the woods and roadsides with ghostlike clouds. For many Islanders this is the most beautiful and long anticipated event of the Vineyard spring, and once the shadbush has bloomed you know that spring is here to stay. The vision is as fleeting as it is ethereal, and soon the shadbush trees and Juneberry bushes, which bloom about a week later, are covered with clusters of small slightly pear-shaped fruit which turns dark red by late June. While people are searching high and low for blueberries they pass by bush after bush of shad and Juneberry, not realizing that they are missing one of the Vineyard's most delicious wild berries. The Indians and early settlers appreciated the abundance of these berries and gathered them along with the blueberries to be used in much the same way, fresh or dried, in pies and preserves. The blooming of the shadbush usually coincided with the running of the shad in the Island streams, hence the name shad bush. It is also known to some as wild pear.

Description   Slender tree 6' - 15', or bush 4' - 10' (Juneberry). Bark gray, often mottled with lighter gray spots. Leaves oval, toothed margins. Flower white, 5 petals. Berries pear-shaped, reddish purple, on long stems in drooping clusters of 3 or 4 berries.

Location   Wooded areas throughout Island, roadsides.

Dates edible   July.

Preparation   Berries: Fresh, jams, jellies, dried etc. Use like blueberries. (See recipe page 85).

49

BURDOCK - *Arctium lappa*

This is another troublesome weed that is a delicious vegetable - if you want to go to the trouble of gathering it. The roots of the first-year plant of the biennial burdock are edible, but they can be two or three feet long and four inches wide and hard work to dig up. It is grown commercially in Japan and Hawaii, and imported, canned burdock roots sell for exorbitant prices in epicurean stores in the cities. This is the plant that bears the round, brown burrs that catch onto your socks and sweaters when you walk through fields in the fall and winter.

Description Large, sprawling, biennial plant, 1'- 4'. First-year plant resembles rhubarb plant. Leaves large; basal leaves up to 1½' wide, egg-shaped with tapering tip. Flowers purple, resemble thistle flowers.

Location Waste places, farmyards, fields.

Dates edible May to July.

Preparation Roots (of first-year plant; plant has no flower stalk): Boiled. To prepare, clean and peel root. Slice thin and boil 40 min. with pinch of baking soda. Flower stalk (gather before flowers form): Boiled. Must be peeled. (See recipe page 82).

Medicinal properties Root: General tonic; increases flow of urine; applied externally as salve for burns, skin irritations. "...the roots themselves given to drink with old wine, doth wonderfully help the biting of serpents; the root beaten with a little salt and laid on the place suddenly easeth the pain thereof, and helpeth those that are bitten by a mad dog..." - Culpeper.

CATBRIER - *Smilax rotundifolia*

Catbrier grows virtually everywhere on the Vineyard from the edges of beaches to abandoned fields and farmyards. It is a thorn-bearing vine which climbs over other vegetation, often forming prickly impenetrable patches. The tender furled leaves and tendrils at the tips of the vines make delicious salad greens and are tasty just to nibble on raw as you walk through the woods.

Description Climbing, thorn-bearing vine. Stems slender, woody, green, curling tendrils. Leaves heart-shaped with pointed tip, leathery, 2″ - 3″. Flowers inconspicuous, green, bell-shaped. Berries blue-black, in clusters.

Location All over Island, fields, roadsides, woods.

Dates edible May to July.

Preparation Tender, furled leaves and tendrils at tips of vines: Raw in salads and sandwiches; potherb. (See recipe page 84).

Medicinal properties Tips of vines: General tonic; increases flow of urine.

Uses Berries: Natural dye, purples, blues.

Catbrier

51

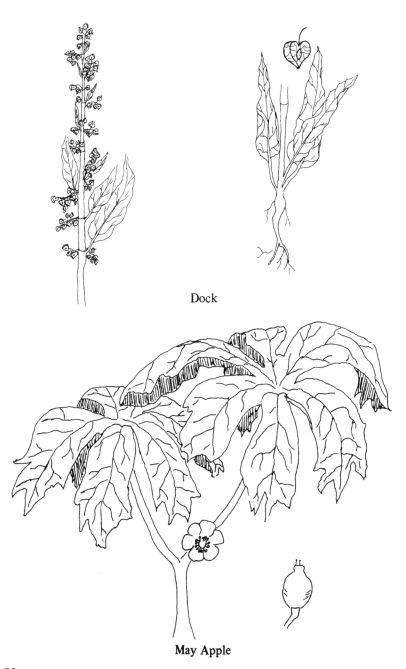

Dock

May Apple

DOCK - *Rumex crispus*

Curly-leaved dock is a weed of the roadsides and fields. It is a delicious spring green even higher in vitamins A and C than carrots and oranges. It has therefore always played an important role in herbal medicine, especially the root which is also high in iron. It is a rather undistinguished-looking plant until the fall when its single flower stalk bears many rich brown, winged seeds which the birds love and Vineyarders collect to use in dried flower arrangements.

Description Smooth dark green plant, 1' - 3'. Leaves narrow with curly margins, mostly basal. Flowers greenish, in whorls or hanging clusters at top of flower stalk. Seeds brown, winged, numerous. Roots bright yellow.

Location Waste places, roadsides.

Dates edible April to mid-May.

Preparation First leaves in spring: Potherb. (See recipes page 84).

Medicinal properties Root: Listed in U. S. Dispensatory. Laxative; general tonic; astringent; applied to skin irritations.

MAY APPLE - *Podophyllum peltatum*

This impressive and exotic-looking plant is rare on the Vineyard and should not be picked for eating. I have included it because it is a fascinating plant and you do occasionally run across large patches of it on the Island. The fruit of the May apple is edible when ripe, but the rest of the plant, especially the root, is extremely poisonous. The roots contain the active principle podophyllus, a powerful drug used in treating kidney and liver ailments, but which can cause death in overdose. The plant was used extensively by Indians and early settlers for both medicinal and malicious purposes.

Description 1' - 3'. Stem rounded, forked, each branch supports one leaf. Leaves large, umbrella-shaped, 1' or more across. Flower petals, fleshy, cream-colored, borne at fork in stem. Fruit yellow, egg-shaped.

Location Heavy, moist woods.

Dates edible September.

Preparation Fruit: Raw, jams, jellies.

Medicinal properties Root: Regulates liver and bowels; cure for chronic liver and kidney problems, jaundice, uterine diseases. Poisonous in overdose.

53

Jerusalem Artichoke

JERUSALEM ARTICHOKE - *Helianthus tuberosus*

Jerusalem artichoke is a tall, attractive member of the Sunflower family with edible tubers. The tubers were a staple in the diet of the Indians on the Vineyard who cultivated huge fields of artichokes. Early settlers realized the value of this plant and began shipping it back to Europe where it became very popular. The name Jerusalem is a misinterpretation of the Spanish name for the plant, Girasol, meaning "turning to face the sun," a characteristic of the blossoms of all members of the Sunflower family. The origin of the inappropriate term artichoke is obscure. The potato-like tubers contain no starch and would be a healthy and inexpensive substitute for potatoes in most people's diets. With the recent boom in the local pig population, at least one Island garden is being planted with a few acres of Jerusalem artichokes for pig feed.

Description Tall, hairy plant, 3' - 10'. Resembles common sunflower, but smaller, stalks more slender. Grows in large patches. Flowers resemble sunflowers but are smaller and lack the large, central, seedbearing disk.

Location Fields, wasteplaces.

Dates edible October to April. Gather after first frost.

Preparation Root tubers: Raw, cooked like potato. (See recipes pages 82, 83).

DAY LILY - *Hemerocallis fulva*

This showy member of the Lily family grows both in Island gardens and wild along roadsides and fields. When you come across a patch of day lilies it is tempting to strip off all the usable flowers and buds, but the first rule of gathering any wild food is to take only as much as you need. Leave some behind for others to enjoy. You need not worry about destroying the plant when you gather the edible root tubers. If the de-tubered plant is placed carefully back into the ground, it should grow a new crop of tubers within six weeks. The other wild lilies that grow on the Vineyard are not to be gathered for eating. Most of them have black spots which distinguish them from the day lily.

Description 2' - 4'. Flower orange, 6 petals. Leaves flattened, sword-shaped.

Location Roadsides, fields, gardens.

Dates edible June to September.

Preparation Flowers: Used as in Oriental cooking, in soups, as flavoring, dipped in egg batter. Unopened buds (select mature ones tinged with orange): Sautéed in butter, steamed, in tempura. Day-old flowers: Seasoning in soups. Developing central leaf stalk (gather before flower stalk appears): Peeled, raw in salads, cooked like asparagus. Root tubers: Raw, boiled. Flowers and buds may be dried and stored for winter use. Soak dried products before using them.

WILD SPEARMINT, WILD PEPPERMINT
Mentha spicata, Mentha piperita

There are many edible members of the Mint family on the Vineyard. The two discussed here were probably brought over from England by the early settlers for their herb gardens, and they escaped and quickly naturalized themselves to the conditions in the wilds of America.

Description Resembles garden mint, 1'-5'. Stem square, smooth, usually unbranched until top third. Leaves oval, tapering. Flowers pink to purple, stamens protruding, in terminal whorls. Main difference between spearmint and peppermint is difference in their characteristic fragrances.

Location Damp areas, along streams, ponds, lowlying farmland.

Dates edible May to September.

Preparation Leaves: Jelly, jam, flavoring, in salads, garnish, tea. (See recipes page 83).

Medicinal properties Leaves (listed in U. S. Pharmacopoeia): Remedy for colds, chills, upset stomach, heartburn; flavoring for medicines; antispasmodic. "It is applied with salt to the bitings of mad dogs." - Gerard.

Wild Peppermint   Wild Spearmint

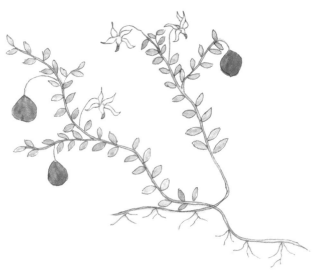

WILD CRANBERRIES - *Vaccinium macrocarpon*

The Indians of Martha's Vineyard not only used most of the available wild edible plants, but also cultivated a great number of them. Perhaps the most successfully cultivated plant was the cranberry. Bogs were tended all over the Island, yielding hundreds of pounds of cranberries a year. Cranberries were easily dried and preserved for winter use as a high source of vitamin C. The Gay Head Indians still hold one of the largest of these bogs as Indian common ground and have a cranberry picking day every fall. The early settlers soon saw the value of this small plant and until fifty years ago many Island farms had small cranberry bogs. However, cranberries have very demanding growing conditions, and most Vineyard farmers eventually found cranberry growing on a small scale impractical. If you come across an abandoned cranberry bog you will generally still find cranberries growing, and there are many places on the Island where they can be found in their totally wild state. Cranberries were originally called craneberries because the delicate flower, with its protruding flower-parts and turned-back petals, bears a resemblance to a crane's head with its swept-back tuft of feathers.

Description Delicate creeping plant. Leaves alternate, small, oval, whitened beneath. Flowers pale pink, nodding, with turned-back petals, protruding flower-parts. Berries red.

Location Bogs, moist low land, often behind dunes.

Dates edible September to October.

Preparation Berries: Use like commercial cranberries. (See recipe page 85).

Uses Berries: Natural dye, red.

58

VIOLETS - *Viola papilionacaea and related species*

One of the prettiest wild edible foods, the violet is also higher in vitamins C and A than any domestic green. Violet flowers are infertile and seldom produce seeds, this job being carried out by inconspicuous blooms on short stalks at the base of the plant or sometimes underground, called cleistogenous flowers, which never produce petals. Thus, picking the showy purple blossoms does not affect the life cycle of the plant.

Description Beautiful, familiar plant, 2" - 6". Flowers purple or white, pansy-like with protruding spur. Leaves heart-shaped.

Location Rich soil, gardens, lawns, roadsides, woods.

Dates edible May to June.

Preparation New leaves: Raw, potherb. Flowers: Raw, in salads, as garnish, in jams, jellies, syrup, or candied. (See recipe page 83).

Medicinal properties Cure for insomnia, anger, wicked spirits, drunkenness and hangover. Syrup made from flowers (listed in British Pharmacopoeia): Laxative; cough syrup. Leaves: Poultice for burns, bruises, wounds, tumors.

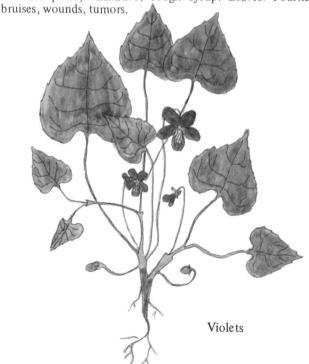

Violets

59

Wintergreen

Wild Onion

WINTERGREEN - *Gaultheria procumbens*

Wintergreen plants grow in abundance in the undergrowth of most of the wooded areas on the Island, and the berries and leaves, both of which taste strongly of wintergreen, are delicious to chew on as you walk through the woods. The berries ripen in the fall and are edible all winter long.

Description Small evergreen plant spreading by creeping stolons, 1" - 3". Leaves stiff, shiny, oval, dark green; new leaves often bright red. Flowers white to pink, bell-shaped, waxy. Berries bright red.

Location Undergrowth in woods. Open moors in Gay Head and Chappaquiddick.

Dates edible Year around.

Preparation Berries: Raw, candied, jams, jellies, etc. Leaves: Tea. To prepare, let leaves soak in covered jar of water overnight to strengthen flavor. Do not boil.

Medicinal properties Leaves (listed in U. S. Pharmacopoeia 1820-1894, essential oil from leaves still listed - contains Methyl salicylate, similar to aspirin): Relieves pain, rheumatism; increases flow of urine; stimulant.

WILD ONION - *Allium species*

There are three types of wild onions found on the Vineyard; all are edible and similar in appearance, though they differ in taste. One of these, *A. Vineale,* is a strong-odored weed which grows in most fields on the Vineyard - cows often feed on it and it imparts a distinct garlic taste to their milk.

Description Resembles garden onion, 6" - 3'. Leaves thin, tubular, resemble chives in spring. Flower stalk appears in July bearing loose terminal cluster of bell-shaped purple-white flowers.

Location Lawns, fields, roadsides.

Dates edible April to August.

Preparation Bulbs: Use like garden onions. Young shoots: Use like chives. Flower clusters (before buds open): Pickled.

Medicinal properties Bulbs (listed in U. S. Pharmacopoeia): Rid body of worms; clear respiratory tract of phlegm; aid digestion. In World War I in England juice from bulbs was applied to wounds as an antiseptic with swabs of sphagnum moss.

Uses Skins: Natural dye, yellows and oranges.

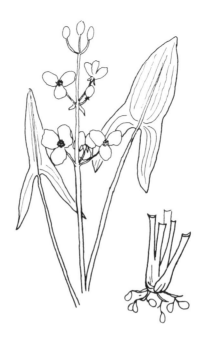

 WAPATOO or ARROWHEAD - *Sagittaria latifolia*

Wapatoo grows in the mud along the edges and in the shallows of fresh-water ponds all over the Island. Its edible tubers were once an important food of the Indians who would wade into the water and root up the tubers with their toes. The women were sent out into the deeper water to hang from the edges of the canoes and comb the bottom. Wapatoo tubers must be dug up as they are lodged firmly in the mud and will only break off if you try to pull up the whole plant. Wapatoo harvesting season comes in October after the leaves have fallen from the plant, and as the waters on the Vineyard can be a bit chilly at that time it is a good idea to bring along a pair of waders, a bucket to catch the tubers as they float to surface, and a clamming fork, rather than trying the Indian method.

Description Large, fleshy plant, 1' - 4'. Leaves arrow-shaped on long stalks. Flowers white, filmy, 3 petals, grow in whorls of 3's on central flower stalk.

Location Edges and shallows of fresh water ponds.

Dates edible September to April.

Preparation Tubers: Use like potatoes.

62

JEWELWEED - *Impatiens capensis*

Jewelweed is best known for its use as a cure for poison ivy. If the juice from the succulent stems of the plant is rubbed onto an area which has been recently exposed to poison ivy, chances are that the itchy rash will never develop. If you already have poison ivy, rub the affected area with jewelweed (it is easiest just to crush the whole plant between your hands to get the juice) and it will work as effectively as any store-bought lotion to dry and heal the rash. The shoots of jewelweed are edible in the early spring, although many sources claim that the plant is poisonous. So it is probably best to exercise caution when you first try jewelweed shoots, as it may adversely affect some people. Jewelweed grows in damp ground all over the Island, often conveniently in the same areas where poison ivy thrives. It bears beautiful cone-shaped yellow flowers with pale orange spots and slipper-shaped pods which, when ripe, explode violently if they are lightly touched, hence the other common name, touch-me-not. The plant itself has succulent translucent stems and resembles an *Impatiens,* a common house plant of the same family.

Description Tall, succulent, tender plant, 1' - 5'. Stems much branched, succulent, translucent, pale-green. Leaves egg-shaped with pointed tip, wavy margin. Flowers yellow with orange mottling, cone-shaped. Seed pods slipper-shaped, when ripe burst open if lightly touched.

Location Moist ground, around ponds and swamps, low-lying farmland.

Dates edible May to early June.

Preparation Young shoots (gather until 4"): Cook like asparagus.

Medicinal properties Juice from stems: Poison ivy antidote; cure for athlete's foot, itchy scalp.

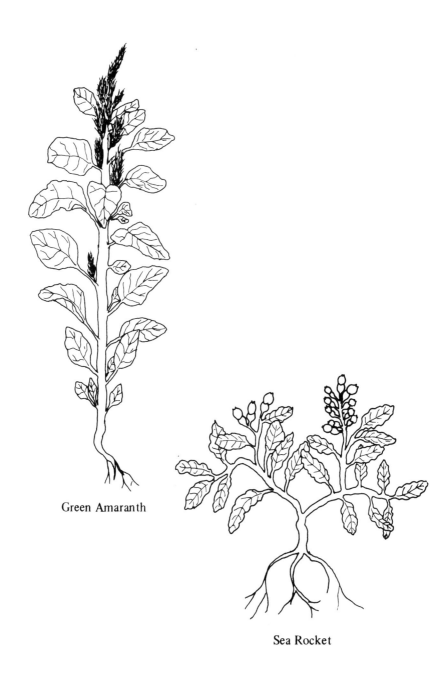

Green Amaranth

Sea Rocket

GREEN AMARANTH - *Amaranthus retroflexus*

Green amaranth is an unattractive coarse plant native to the tropics which grows in almost every Vineyard garden. It can grow up to six feet high and is easily identified by its bright pink root.

Description Stout, unbranching plant, 1' - 6'. Stem hairy. Leaves rough, oval with tapering tips, wavy margins, on leaf stalks the same length as the leaf. Flowers green, chaffy, in spikes. Seeds shiny, black, in spikes. Root bright pink.

Location Gardens, waste places.

Dates edible May to August.

Preparation Leaves of young plant (up to 8") and tender tips of new leaves: Potherb. Seeds: Ground for flour, roasted.

SEA ROCKET - *Cakile edulenta*

The leaves of the beach-growing sea rocket have a distinct horseradish flavor which livens up any salad or picnic sandwich.

Description Fleshy green plant, texture of domestic rubber plant, 3" - 2'. Leaves roughly oval, wavy margins, characteristic horseradish smell when broken. Flowers yellow, inconspicuous. Seed pods egg-shaped, bulbous.

Location Beaches above high water line.

Dates edible May to September.

Preparation New leaves: Raw, potherb.

 FIDDLEHEADS - *Peteridum and Pteretis species*

Fiddleheads are the young developing fronds of ferns which are still tightly coiled in the spring, resembling the tuning head of a fiddle. They are a well-known delicacy and are sold canned and frozen in the cities. Gathering fiddleheads is a joy as it takes you into the Vineyard woods when they are most beautiful, moist and fragrant from the spring rains. While looking for the fiddleheads, you cannot help but notice the deep purple violets and delicate white wood anemones breaking through the brown carpet of rotting leaves and the thick, bright green mounds of moss. Gather fiddleheads while they are still tightly curled and no higher than about six inches, for although all the ferns on the Island are edible at the fiddlehead stage, some become slightly toxic as they mature. Take care when you pick them to break off only the tender, edible coil and not to disturb the rooting system.

Description Curled frond of developing fern, 1" - 6". Covered with rusty gray fuzz.

Location Woods, along streams and ponds, moist rich soil, shaded areas.

Dates edible April to May.

Preparation Steamed, sautéed, raw in salads. Remove fur-like covering before cooking.

Uses Ferns: Natural dye, beige and gray. Fern spores: Magic potion for invisibility.

JAPANESE KNOTWEED - *Polygonum cuspidatum*

Knotweed is a versatile, wild edible plant - it can be treated both as a fruit and as a vegetable with equally delicious results. Knotweed was first brought to this country as an ornamental plant. It is quite attractive, resembling a large-leafed bamboo and growing in graceful, shady bamboo-like patches. However, it established itself so well, spreading rapidly and monopolizing any area in which it grew, that people now tend to regard it as an obnoxious weed, difficult to eradicate.

Description   Tall bamboo-like plant, 4' -12'. Leaves large, ovoid with sharp tip. Stalks hollow, jointed, resemble bamboo, branched, remain standing all winter. Flowers greenish white, in hanging clusters. Seeds brown, winged, in hanging clusters.

Location   Waste places, roadsides, vacant lots.

Dates edible   May to June.

Preparation   New shoots (resemble asparagus, gather until 1'): Cook like asparagus. Young stalks (up to 3'): Use like rhubarb. Purple-green, mottled rind must first be peeled off.

67

JACK-IN-THE-PULPIT - *Arisaema triphyllum*

This beautiful little plant with its distinctive hooded flower and the small minister standing in his "pulpit" is one of the controversial wild edible plants. It is known that the Indians relied heavily on this plant for food, earning it the other common name of Indian turnip. The controversy is over how to prepare it. The root contains microscopic crystals of oxalate of lime, which can cause painful burning of the mouth and throat. Most sources say that the burning crystals can only be broken down by prolonged drying, for about five months, of the thinly sliced roots. The Jack-in-the-Pulpit is not widespread on the Vineyard and should only be gathered when it is found growing in large patches.

Description   Two leaf and one flower stalks arising from basal root bulb, 1' - 3'. Leaves stalked, 3 oval, pointed leaflets. Flowers green and purple striped, with curved canopy-like hood, tubular base, inner fleshy spike of minute flowers. Berries bright red, in egg-shaped cluster.

Location   Moist, low woodlands.

Dates edible   May to September.

Preparation   Roots: Sliced and dried for approx. 5 months, then toasted, boiled, or ground for flour.

Medicinal properties   Freshly dried root (listed in U. S. Pharmacopoeia 1820-1883): Relieves coughs and asthma; promotes perspiration. Indians rubbed powdered root on the temples to relieve headache.

WILD RASPBERRIES - *Rubus species*

There are several kinds of wild raspberries found on the Vineyard. Like the blackberries, raspberry plants are extremely variable in appearance, and to most people there is a constant question of whether a bush is a black raspberry or a blackberry or a dewberry or a wineberry and so forth. It does not really matter, they are all edible and delicious.

Description   Extremely variable. Branching canes usually reddish green, covered with sharp bristles, 1' - 6'. Leaves variable, often compound, 3 - 7 leaflets, or single maple-leaf shape. Flowers pink or white.

Location   Thickets, open fields, roadsides.

Dates edible   July to August.

Preparation   Berries: Fresh, in jams, jellies, wine, etc. New shoots (in May): Peeled, raw in salads. (See recipe page 85).

Medicinal properties   Leaves (thoroughly dried): For diarrhea; as gargle for sore throat and mouth; astringent. Dried leaves, mixed with cream: suppress vomiting.

Jack-in-the-Pulpit

Wild Raspberries

MUSHROOMS

Sulphur or chicken mushroom

Polyporous Arcularius

There are many choice edible mushrooms found on the Vineyard and some Islanders gather hundreds of pounds of them during the summer to use fresh and to dry for winter use. There are also many poisonous mushrooms on the Vineyard, and so no one who does not know exactly what he is doing should pick mushrooms for eating without experienced guidance. I

Boletus   *Boletus edulis*

Morel   *Morchella esculenta*

Meadow mushroom   *Agaricus campestris*

Shaggy mane   *Coprinus comatus*

have mentioned a few of the most common edible ones, but I have not attempted to describe them. To quote an ancient herbalist, "To conclude, few of them are good to be eaten, and most do suffocate and strangle the eater. Therefore I give my advice unto those that do love such strange and new fangled meates, to beware of licking honey among thorns, least the sweetnesse of the one do not countervaile the sharpnesse and pricking of the other." (See recipes pages 83, 84).

Inky cap *Coprinus micaceus*

Parasol mushroom *Lepiota procera*

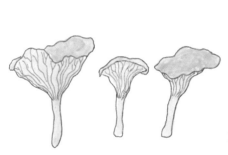

Chantrelle *Cantherellus cibarius*

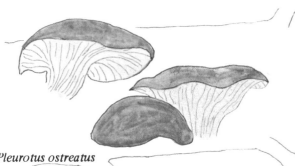

Oyster mushroom *Pleurotus ostreatus*

WILD ASPARAGUS - *Asparagus officinale*

Wild asparagus is identical with garden asparagus and may be gathered and prepared in the same way. To locate a patch of wild asparagus look for the feathery stalk of the fully grown asparagus which usually towers over the other vegetation around it. In the winter the asparagus plant will turn brown but remain standing to mark the place where new shoots will appear in the spring.

Description   Identical with garden asparagus. Fully grown plant is bushy and much branched. Leaves thread-like. Flowers green, bell-shaped. Berries red.

Location   Roadsides, edges of fields.

Dates edible   Late May to June.

Preparation   Young shoots: Like garden asparagus.

Medicinal properties   Laxative; increases flow of urine; promotes perspiration. "The root in the spring time, steeped in wine, doth give it a delicate flavor and taste, and being drunk fasting every morning comforteth the heart, and is a good preservative against the plague or any other poison." - Culpeper.

BLACKBERRIES, DEWBERRIES - *Rubus species*

Fall, winter and spring everyone curses the brambles and vines that catch and tear your ankles and clothes when you go walking in Island fields and thickets. By mid-summer you whistle a different tune; the obnoxious brambles are covered with juicy ripe blackberries. But if you happen to find any blackberries as late as October first, don't pick them, as from that date on, according to an old English tale, the Devil spits on them.

Description   Extremely variable. Can be prickly bush up to 10' or trailing vine. Leaves pinnate, 3 to 9 leaflets with toothed margins. Flower attractive, white, 5 petals, many stamens.

Location   Sunny fields, thickets, waste places.

Dates edible   July to August.

Preparation   Berries: Fresh, jellies, jams, wine, etc. New shoots (gather when approx. 2"): Raw in salads. Must be peeled. (See recipes pages 84, 85).

Medicinal properties   Roots, leaves: Rich in tannin. General tonic; relieve diarrhea; sweeten breath; astringent; "excellent good lotions for sores in the mouth or secret parts". - Culpeper. Berries: Relieve diarrhea; "...powerful remedy against the poison of the most venomous serpents." - Culpeper. Leaves boiled in lye: "...head washed therein healeth the itch and running sores thereof and maketh the hair black." - Culpeper.

Uses   Berries: Natural dye, brownish purples. Vines: Natural dye, red tans.

73

HOPS - *Humulus lupulus*

Hops, identical with those cultivated for brewing beer and ale, grow wild on the Vineyard. The cone-like fruiting bodies, the "hops", can be used in brewing in the same manner as cultivated hops, and the young shoots of the plant make an excellent potherb. Hops were once extensively employed in both America and Europe as an effective sedative.

Description   Climbing vine. Leaves opposite, heart-shaped, toothed margins. Female flowers borne in cone-like fruiting bodies, the "hops". Male flowers in loosely hanging clusters.

Location   Open thickets, meadows. Often climbing up the sides of barns.

Dates edible   Shoots: May to June. Hops: September to October.

Preparation   Shoots (gather until 4"): Boiled. Change water once. Hops: Used in brewing.

Medicinal properties   Hops (listed in U. S. Pharmacopoeia 1831-1916): Contain lupulin which is a sedative and hypnotic drug. Sedative. Increases flow of urine. In Europe, sleeping on a pillow filled with hops was said to calm the nerves, cure insomnia and prevent nightmares.

Uses   Stems: Made into fiber. Hops: As yeast substitute in bread making; oil expressed for use as perfume base.

CHICKWEED - *Stellaria media*

In a mild winter chickweed can be gathered all year round on the Vineyard. Even during the coldest winters, you can find tired-looking chickweed plants bravely putting out a few flowers on warm days in January. Chickweed is an inconspicuous plant except in the early spring when it spreads over lawns and gardens in large mats bearing hundreds of tiny white flowers.

Description   Small, pale-green, inconspicuous plant. Seldom grows more than 2″ off the ground, but may spread in mats 2′ to 3′ wide. Stems succulent, much branched, slightly swollen at leaf-joints. Leaves opposite, egg-shaped with sharp tip. Flowers small, white, star-shaped, 5 deeply cleft petals.

Location   Waste places, lawns, roadsides, gardens.

Dates edible   April to September.

Preparation   New stalks and leaves: Raw, potherb. Often combined with other greens as it is bland-tasting. (See recipe page 84).

Medicinal properties   Potherb: High vitamin content. Eaten in early spring, folk method for ridding body of excess weight gained over the winter. Relieves constipation and any form of internal inflammation. Poultice of plant: Clears boils, inflammations, abscesses, itching.

OTHER WILD PLANTS TO BE USED AS TEAS

Gather leaves and flowers for teas just before the plant blooms or while in bloom for maximum flavor and medicinal value. Dry them in a warm room away from the sun. All of the teas mentioned here are worth drinking for their good taste as well as their medicinal properties.

Goldenrod - *Solidago odora:* Tastes like anise. Promotes sweating; clears stomach.

Catnip - *Nepta cataria:* The plant cats love. High in vitamins A and C. Induces sleep and prevents nightmares.

Gill-over-the-ground - *Glechoma hederacea:* Use fresh herb. Stimulates appetite. Clears cough. High in vitamin C. Destroys lead accumulated in body. Used as substitute for hops in brewing.

Wild Thyme - *Thymus serpyllum:* Relieves cough and fever. Induces sleep. Cures hangover if taken with pinch of salt. Used as flavoring.

Sweet Fern - *Comptonia peregrina:* Cures diarrhea. Rids body of worms.

Water Mint - *Mentha arvensis:* Similar to peppermint.

Red Clover Blossoms - *Trifolium praetense:* Clears coughs.

Boneset - *Eupatorium perfoliatum:* Clears fevers. Stimulates appetite. Relieves rheumatism.

Yarrow - *Achillea millefolium:* Relieves fever. Purifies blood. Plant used to conjure Devil; ground for a love charm.

RECIPES

Methods For Preserving Grape Leaves   Mrs. Sophie Block, West Tisbury

Clip large quantity of fairly large grape leaves before they grow tough. Wash in cold water. Tie loosely in packs of 30-40. Blanch for few seconds in large pan of boiling water with ½ cup salt. When they turn yellowish green, remove, drain, wrap in foil and freeze. Following the above method, instead of freezing the leaves, they also may be sealed tightly into sterilized jars with a bit of the brine added. Ready in one week. Will keep for months.

Yerba - Using Wild Grape Leaves   Mrs. Sophie Block, West Tisbury

2 pks. grape leaves

1 lb. ground lamb or beef

½ cup raw rice

Ground pepper

2 tbls. Worcestershire sauce

½ tsp. cinnamon

2-3 tbls. chopped mint leaves

½ tsp. allspice

1 tsp. salt

20-30 apricots

Juice of 1 lemon

1 tsp. sugar

¼ cup water

Wash leaves to remove salt. Mix meat, spices and rice with Worcestershire sauce. Stuff leaves using 1 tbls. per leaf. Arrange in shallow casserole. Place apricots between leaves. Pour water, lemon juice and mint over leaves. Cover and bake at 350° for 35-45 min. Add more water if necessary.

Beach Plum Wine   Lynn and Jim Blaine, Edgartown

Makes 1 gallon (dry, deep rose)

3-4 lbs. ripe beach plums

2½ lbs. sugar

1 tsp. acid blend

1 tsp. yeast nutrient

1 tsp. Montrachet wine yeast

½ tsp. pectic enzyme powder

1 Campden tablet

Crush beach plums, put in plastic 2-gallon bucket, crock, or stainless steel pot. Boil sugar in ½ gallon of water. Allow to cool. Dissolve Campden tablet in a little water. Add sugar water and Campden solution to beach plums; cover tightly with plastic wrap; let sit 24 hours. Then add the other ingredients. Ferment in warm place 5-6 days, stirring daily with sterilized wooden spoon. Then strain and press out juice; put in gallon jug, adding water to fill if necessary. Fit jug with fermentation lock. Rack in 3 weeks, again in 3 months. (Racking means siphoning the clear wine off the sediment, and returning the wine to clean jug.) After about 3 or 4 months the sugar should be fermented out, and the wine will be very dry, but if you prefer it a little sweet, you can stop the fermentation whenever you like by adding a crushed Campden tablet. This kills the yeast.

Rose Petal Candy

Blend freshly picked rose petals in blender with small amount of water to consistency of thick paste. Add ½ to 1 pint of heavy cream, mix well. Remove from blender and slowly add sifted confectioner's sugar until the whole thing is a heavy paste. Spread out on a large plate and refrigerate. This will make an extremely sweet but delicious candy much like a sweet you would be served in India.

Rose Petal Jam

Place freshly picked rose petals in a bowl and cover them with a layer of sugar. Let sit for a few days. Blend soggy petals in blender and add more sugar until reaches jam-like consistency. Refrigerate.

Rose Petal Syrup

Dry rose petals thoroughly in sun. Chop fine by hand or in blender. Make a syrup of equal parts of sugar and water and add the petals when syrup reaches 215°. Stir well and pour into sterilized jar. Use like honey, on bread or pancakes, etc.

Cake Flavoring

Turn out a freshly baked cake still hot onto porous surface covered with rose petals, mint leaves, or golden rod leaves to cool. The cake will absorb their flavor.

Uncooked Rosehip Purée

Lynn and Jim Blaine, Edgartown

4 cups seeded rosehips
2 tbls. lemon juice

A little honey or sugar to taste
Enough water to permit blending

Run it through your blender, pour into containers and freeze. Tastes great with yogurt or on toast.

4 oz. of hips from *rosa rugosa* contains 2275 to 6977 milligrams of vitamin C. One handful of hips is equivalent to about 60 oranges. Since heat destroys some of the vitamin C, I don't cook this; instead I freeze it. (Raw rosehips don't lose an appreciable amount of vitamin C in the freezer for up to 6 months).

Rosehip Wine

Lynn and Jim Blaine, Edgartown

Makes 5 gallons delicious, amber, sherry-like wine

20 lbs. rosehips (no need to seed them)
10 oz. orange juice
13 lbs. granulated sugar
1 tbls. citric acid powder

1 package Montrachet wine yeast
Campden tablets for sterilizing
 (Sears has them)
1 tbls. pectic enzyme
1 package yeast nutrient

Wash the rosehips. If you don't have a crusher, smash them a few at a time in a bucket with a sledge hammer. Put them in a 10 gallon plastic trashcan along with the orange juice. Boil half the sugar in 2½ gallons of water; cool somewhat. Dissolve 5 Campden tablets in a little water. Add the sugar water and Campden solution to the rosehips and stir. (The sterilizer, which eventually dissipates, is to kill any foreign yeasts on the rose hips.) Cover pail with plastic wrap (taped on) and let it sit for 24 hours. Then add the citric acid powder, wine yeast, pectic enzyme, and the yeast nutrient. Again cover tightly. Ferment in warm place for 5-6 days, stirring daily. (Be sure all your equipment is sterilized with some more Campden solution.) After 5 or 6 days, strain out solids and press in wine press or put in sterile pillowcase and keep squeezing and twisting it to get all the juice out. Put the liquid in a sterile 5-gallon jug. Boil the remaining 6½ lbs. sugar in about 2 gallons of water. Cook to lukewarm and add to jug. If jug isn't quite full, add more water. Put a fermentation lock on the jug. Rack in 3 weeks, and again in 3 months. (Racking means siphoning the clear wine off the sediment, cleaning the jug, and putting the wine back in.) It takes several months until it's through fermenting. After bottling, let it age at least 6 months. This will be a dry wine when it is through fermenting, but if you want it to be sweet, you can stop the fermentation by adding 1 crushed Campden tablet per gallon. This kills the yeast.

Beach Peas Louise Tate King, The Martha's Vineyard Cook Book, West Tisbury

Vegetable steamer
2½ cups shelled beach peas
½ tsp. salt
1 tsp. sugar

½ cup medium cream
Freshly ground black pepper
1 tbls. chopped fresh chives (optional)
4 tbls. butter

Place the steamer and about an inch of water in a saucepan, cover and bring water to a boil. Put peas in steamer, cover pot, and steam about 10 minutes. Remove steamer and peas from pan, pour out water, replace peas and add all other ingredients except chives. Simmer over low heat for 5 minutes, stirring once or twice. Do not boil. Serve hot with chives sprinkled on top and an additional dusting of black pepper. (3 to 4 portions).

Note: You might like to try cooking beach peas like snow peas - leaving them in the pods for steaming. In this case, the tedium of shelling would be eliminated, but the peas have to be gathered when very young.

Elder Flower Vinegar Old Cook Book

Fill wide mouth jar loosely with elderberry flowers picked fresh and spread in warming pan to dry through. Cover with any vinegar and stand jar in sun for half a day. Strain through flannel, bottle and cork tight.

Spiced Elderberries Old Cook Book

To 9 lbs. berries add 1 pint vinegar. Put in granite kettle and bring to boil. Boil 10 mins. and stir in 3 lbs. white sugar and 3 grated nutmegs. Stir constantly until cooked down to consistency of jam, then put in jars and seal. Makes excellent filling for winter pies.

Pickled Elderberry Buds Old Cook Book

Gather buds while firm, cover with a strong brine and let stand a week, stirring 2 or 3 times a day. Then strain from brine, put in a granite kettle, cover with a few grape leaves, pour brine back on and let simmer 3 hours. Drain and put in bottles. Take enough wine vinegar to cover and to each quart allow 1 blade mace, 2 minced shallots and a small slice of green ginger. Bring to a boil, boil 5 minutes and strain over buds. Cover and seal.

Elderberry Flower Fritters

Pick the elderberry blossoms while they are still covered with dew. Gently dry them and trim off the tough stems.

1 cup flour
2 tbls. sugar
½ tsp. salt
1 tsp. baking powder

2 eggs
½ - ¾ cup milk

1 tsp. melted butter

Sift together the dry ingredients. Mix the well-beaten eggs, milk and melted butter together and gently stir in the dry ingredients. Dip the flower heads in the batter, shaking off excess. Deep fry in light oil for 3 to 5 minutes until golden brown. Drain on paper towels. Sprinkle with orange or lemon juice, nutmeg and sugar. Serve immediately.

Seaweed Pudding

Bring to near boil 1 quart to ½ gallon of milk (depending on size of mold). Add a large handful of cleaned Irish moss. Heat at near boil for 20-30 mins., stirring frequently, until most of the Irish moss has dissolved. Pour through a strainer into a large bowl, pushing through as much of the partly dissolved Irish moss as possible. Discard the larger, undissolved pieces. (The more the Irish moss has dissolved, the firmer the pudding will be.) Add flavoring and sweetening to taste. Vanilla, orange juice, mashed peaches, nutmeg, cinnamon, maple syrup, honey make a good combination, as do vanilla, ground chocolate, sugar and orange juice. Pour into a mold and set in refrigerator until firm. Garnish with fresh fruit when served.

Candied Sassafras Root

Make a heavy sugar syrup out of 2 parts sugar to 1 part water. Heat, stirring constantly until reaches rolling boil. Boil for a bit. Add finely grated sassafras root and remove from heat. Spread on a plate and place in refrigerator to cool.

Dandelion Salad

Cut a 2" square of real bacon into small chunks and fry until done. Set aside bacon and throw out half of the bacon grease (more or less depending on how much there is and how many dandelion greens you have). Briefly sauté some chopped sweet Bermuda onion in the pan till barely tender. Toss onions, bacon grease and bacon chunks with cleaned dandelion greens. Serve immediately. Add a bit of Feta cheese if you like. No need for vinegar as the greens are tart enough.

Dandelion Bud Omelet
Louise Tate King, The Martha's Vineyard Cook Book

12 dandelion buds

4 eggs

About 3 tbls. butter

½ tsp. salt

Freshly ground black pepper

Pick dandelion buds just about to open; wash them if necessary, and toss them in paper towels to dry. Melt 2 tbls. butter in small skillet or omelet pan, add dandelion buds, and cook them slowly 2 or 3 minutes, stirring carefully so they will cook on all sides. Remove the pan from heat. Take out dandelion buds and reserve. Beat eggs gently only until mixed; stir in salt. Heat pan with additional butter (about 1 tbls.) over moderate heat until butter foams. Pour eggs into pan and cook slowly, lifting around edges to allow uncooked mixture to run under omelet. When eggs are almost done, spoon dandelion buds onto one half of omelet. Fold omelet. Dust lightly with pepper and serve at once. (2 portions).

Dandelion Wine
Isabel M. White of the Scottish Bakehouse, Tisbury

3 gallons dandelion blossoms, tightly packed

1 oz. cake yeast

Juice of 1 doz. lemons

5 lbs. sugar

Water

Gather the blossoms at height of bloom. Be sure to have at least 3 tightly packed gallons. Put in a stone jar and cover with water. Let stand for 2 days. Then boil for 15 minutes. Drain through a sieve, add lemon juice and sugar. Boil at least 10 minutes until sugar is dissolved. Add yeast when cold, either directly or float it on toast. Let stand for 3 weeks then sieve through cheese cloth. Bottle, but don't cork tightly for at least 2 months. Should stand for 6 months before using.

Wild Strawberry Shortcake   Ada Manning, Gay Head

Remove the snuffs from the strawberries (hull them). Wash. Drain.

2 cups flour	½ tsp. salt
¼ cup sugar	
3 tsps. baking powder	2/3 cup lard

Add milk to dry ingredients so mixture is soft but not wet. Take half of the dough and roll out on floured board. Spread it with soft butter. Roll out other half and place on top of first. Place in oven at 400°. Bake for 30 to 40 minutes. Split in half (this will be easy because of the layer of butter). Add sweetened berries and whipped fresh cream.

Yucca   Mrs. Sophie Block, West Tisbury

Use freshly chopped blossoms in a salad.

Roast the fruit while still slightly green. Peel after roasting and use like a sweet potato in dishes such as candied yucca. The fruit when it is ripe is sweet and gummy and very nourishing.

Nettle Soup   Old Cook Book

Wash and cut up nettles. Pour boiling water over, drain and chop to mush. Add meat broth and cook for only few minutes. Tradition has it you will be beautiful if you eat nettles in the spring.

Potent Sumac Liquor   Craig Kingsbury, Tisbury

Steep 2 quarts of sumac berries in 2 quarts of boiling water. Strain through cheese cloth to remove fine hairs. Sweeten to taste. Add 1 lb. raisins to each 4 quarts of mixture. Place in earthenware crock and add one yeast cake to entire batch. Store in warm dark place until bubbling ceases (maybe 4 or 5 days).

Purslane Soup

Sauté 1 cup purslane and 1 tbls. finely chopped spring onions in 1 tbls. butter. Add salt, freshly ground pepper, and chopped fresh parsley. Stir in ½ cup chablis and 4 cups fresh cream. Heat but do not boil. Serve immediately.

Pigweed Soufflé   Sue Whiting, West Tisbury

½ cup butter	¼ tsp. pepper
1 cup sour cream	½ cup grated cheese
½ tsp. dry mustard	
1 cup flour, more or less as necessary	6 eggs separated
1 tsp. salt	12 oz. pigweed steamed and chopped

Prepare as you would any soufflé. Melt butter. Stir in flour. Add sour cream. Add a little milk if necessary. Blend in cheese. Stir this mixture into 1/3 of the beaten egg yolk mixture. Mix thoroughly and add rest of egg yolks. Blend in pigweed. Beat egg whites till stiff and fold them into the mixture. Pour into a soufflé dish placed in a pan of water. Bake at 350° for approximately 40 minutes.

Sorrel Soup   Louise Tate King, The Martha's Vineyard Cook Book, West Tisbury

2 cups sorrel leaves firmly packed
3 tbls. butter
1 medium onion chopped fine (or
   ¾ cup finely chopped green onion)
1 tbl. flour
3 cups chicken stock (canned
   stock may be used)

½ tsp. salt
Freshly ground black pepper
2 egg yolks
2 tbls. chopped parsley (or
   2 tbls. chopped chives)
1 cup medium cream

Prepare the leaves by trimming off the stringy parts. Rinse them and drain thoroughly on paper towels. Chop fine, or use scissors to cut the leaves. Melt the butter in a heavy 2-quart saucepan, add the onion and cook over low heat until golden and transparent. Stir in the flour thoroughly. Stir in the chopped sorrel and cook until the leaves are wilted. Add the chicken stock and salt and pepper and cook until the mixture comes to a simmer. Cook an additional 5 minutes. Beat the egg yolks; gradually beat in the cream. Then slowly beat in two cups of the hot soup. Return this mixture to the soup pot and cook carefully over very low heat, stirring constantly, for another moment or two. Do not boil. Additional salt and pepper may be added. Serve hot or very cold. Garnish with chopped chives or parsley or both.

Scandinavian Chokecherry Soup   Mrs. Sophie Block, West Tisbury
Extract the juice from chokecherries, bring to a boil, and pour immediately into sterilized jars and seal. To prepare the soup, add 1 jar of water to 1 jar of juice and boil for 20 minutes with the juice and rind of 1 lemon and 1 stick of cinnamon. Strain out lemon and cinnamon. Sweeten to taste. Thicken slightly with cornstarch. Boil again to clear. Serve hot or cold as soup or dessert, with a dollop of sour cream and sprinkling of cinnamon for each bowl.

Boiled Burdock With Salt Pork   Ada Manning, Gay Head
To gather root and flowering stalk of first year plant for this dish, dig the plant and peel off (never cut) the leaves and leaf stalks and discard. Cook salt pork or smoked shoulder in boiling water until done. Remove from water and add small potatoes, carrots and sliced burdock root and stalk and boil for 20 minutes.

Jerusalem Artichokes
              Louise Tate King, The Martha's Vineyard Cook Book, West Tisbury

Vegetable steamer (optional)
12-16 Jerusalem artichokes
2 tbls. butter

1 tsp. salt
1 tbls. chopped parsley
Freshly ground black pepper

Wash artichokes well. If dirty from ground, soak in cold water before scrubbing. Trim off tiny rootlets, but do not peel. If disparately shaped, cut into pieces of approximately the same size. Place in steamer over 1 inch of boiling water and steam until tender - 15 to 20 minutes; or boil them in water to cover, approximately the same time. They will suddenly get mushy; test them with a fork from time to time and try not to overcook them. Remove artichokes and steamer (if used) from pan and pour out water. Replace artichokes, add butter, salt, parsley, and pepper. Cut into smaller pieces if desired. Reheat slightly and serve warm. Delicious with roast meat.
Jerusalem artichokes may also be sliced thin, dried and served salted for hors d'oeuvres. Or add thinly sliced Jerusalem artichokes to soups and stews, or use like water chestnuts in chinese cooking. (4 portions).

Jerusalem Artichoke Salad   Craig Kingsbury, Tisbury
Pour boiling salted water over thinly sliced Jerusalem artichokes. Chill and add your favorite salad dressing.

Jerusalem Artichoke Soup   Margaret McKean Vernon, Hamilton, Mass.
Take one pound of Jerusalem artichokes and simmer in a quart of chicken stock until tender. Purée in a blender. Add one pint of cream, a fistful of parsley and some chives and put through the blender a second time. (If it seems too thick add a little milk.) Heat on top of double boiler. Serve hot or well chilled. (Serves 4).

Glazed Violet Flowers, Wild Mint Leaves and Rose Petals
Method 1
Pick leaves and petals while still moist with dew. Dry on paper towels. Mix carefully: 1 egg white slightly beaten and 1½ tsp. water. With a soft small brush, paint each leaf or flower with the mixture, covering the entire surface. Dust thoroughly and gently with superfine sugar. Place on screen to dry. Store in airtight container.

Method 2
Flowers and leaves glazed in this manner will store longer (about 3 months), but some of the more delicate blossoms might not keep their shape as well as in Method 1.
Stir 1 cup sugar in ½ cup water over low heat till clear. Cool slightly and add 4 tsps. powdered acacia. Chill thoroughly. Dip each flower or leaf in this mixture, using a soft paint brush to coat all surfaces totally. Place coated flowers or leaves on rack to dry. Turn gently with a spatula after 10 hours. When thoroughly dry, store in airtight containers.

Pickled Wild Mushrooms   Mrs. Rose Treat, Gay Head
In a small saucepan put sliced mushrooms in a French dressing made with oil and vinegar, garlic and onion, adding whatever herbs you wish. Cook for about ½ an hour. Pour contents into a jar, add nutmeg, or allspice, put in refrigerator and let sit for a few days.
Helpful hints about cooking wild mushrooms:
Different wild mushrooms require different cooking times. Morels will be ready in 3 minutes; chicken mushrooms will cook from 20 to 30 minutes. It is best to do your own experimenting.
You can also sauté mushrooms in oil and butter adding a little curry for ½ an hour or more until they dry like nuts. Or they can be sautéed for up to 8 hours over a very low flame, turning every so often until dry. Serve as hors d'oeuvres.
Add sliced mushrooms to melted butter and a little olive oil. With a pinch of curry and a little lemon juice cook till tender.
Wild sliced mushrooms are also delicious added to Barley Soup during the last ½ hour of cooking.

Mushroom Catsup

Old Cook Book

Gather full-grown mushrooms (*Agaricus campestris* is especially good) on a dry day. Clean thoroughly, and for each peck take 1 cup of salt, putting the mushrooms in a deep dish in layers with salt between. Let stand 4 or 5 hours, then break mushrooms into pieces, set aside in a cool place for 3 days and occasionally stir and mash to extract the juice. Measure the pulp without straining, and to each quart add ¼ ounce cayenne, ½ ounce allspice, ½ ounce ginger and 2 blades ground mace. Put all into a stone jar, cover closely, set in a pan of boiling water and let boil 3 hours. Then put in a saucepan over direct heat, simmer ½ hours and pour into a jug. Set this in a cool place until next day, then pour off liquid gently, leaving all sediment in jug. Strain liquid through a flannel bag and store in clean dry bottles, adding a few drops of brandy to each pint. Cool and seal.

Blackberry Slump

Mrs. Gertrude Turner, West Tisbury

Boil a quart of blackberries with enough water to make a thick sauce and sugar to taste. Drop spoon-size baking powder dumplings into the mixture and boil for 20 minutes.

Wild Green Smoothie

Peter Lombardi, Tisbury

3 cups finely chopped wild greens (chickweed, lamb's-quarters, orach, catbrier tips, sorrel, dried strawberry leaves, dandelion, purslane, violet leaves; any combination)
    Boiling water   Honey
    Orange, pineapple, lemon and apple juice
Cover 2 cups of greens with boiling water. Simmer for 5 minutes. Strain and sweeten to taste. Let cool. Add 2 to 3 cups of fruit juices and mix well. In a blender, mix 1 cup of this mixture with the uncooked cup of greens. Blend well, strain and sweeten. Add to other mixture and chill thoroughly.

Raggedy Ass Stew or Poverty Soup

Craig Kingsbury, Tisbury

Take one pig's jowl, slice, brown and place in a kettle of water. Add plenty of wild garlic, 1 quart of fava beans, a mess of wild greens (pig weed, chicory greens, dandelion greens, dock, mustard greens, pokeweed shoots, etc.), 1 quart ground nuts (hazel nuts, acorns, hickory nuts, etc.) and red pepper to taste.

Herb Pie

Toss 2 hearts of heads of lettuce, fistful of watercress, some parsley, same amount of mustard greens and lamb's-quarters, handful chopped wild onion shoots, and few new beet greens in pot boiling water. Boil furiously for few minutes, drain well, chop fine, season with pepper, paprika, and salt. In separate pan beat two eggs with cup of milk and cup of cream, stir in flour and mix until lumpless batter. Mix with chopped herbs and pour into baking dish and cook in moderate oven until brown crust forms on top. Spread with butter.

Dewberry Tart

Anne Lowell Finnerty, Tea Lane
(from her cookbook "Fêtes Accomplies")

Pâte sablée for 9" crust:

1¼ cups flour	½ cup soft butter
2 egg yolks	½ cup confectioner's sugar
A very little lemon juice	Grated lemon rind

Work butter into flour with finger tips, until resembles fine meal. Sprinkle the paste with the sugar and lemon rind, mix it in. Work in the egg yolks and add a little lemon juice, if necessary to make a good pastry dough that cleans the bowl. Wrap the dough in waxed paper and chill for at least an hour or overnight.

To bake crust, roll out dough to fit pie plate, press into place with finger tips. Prick the crust with a fork and chill for ½ hour. Weight crust down with cup of rice or marbles and bake at 400° for 10 minutes. Reduce temperature to 350° and bake 5 minutes longer, or until crust is golden brown.

Filling:

2 cups dewberries	1-1½ cups currant jelly

Spread berries over the baked crust. Stir jelly with a fork and melt over low heat. Then pour it over the berries. Serve the tart with unsweetened whipped cream. (6 portions).

Fruit Pies

Mix wild berries together for more interesting pies. Blackberries and blueberries are a **good** combination. So are shadberries and blueberries. You might need to make changes in the amount of thickener you use to compensate for the differences in the berries' juiciness. Using dried berries gives an interesting taste change. Elderberries should always be dried before they are used in pies and are good in any combination.

Fish Cooked With Wild Thyme

Cathy Iselin, Tisbury

Spread the bottom of a shallow baking dish with sprigs of wild thyme. Place the fish filets on this and cover with very thinly sliced tomatoes, and a few more sprigs of thyme, and pats of butter. Add a few squeezes of lemon. Bake until flaky. 10 to 15 minutes.

Pickled Chicken Claws

Pick the tender tips of chicken claws and break them into 1 inch pieces. Place in small jars. Make a pickling brine of 2 cups of cider vinegar; 2 cups white vinegar; 3 tbls. pickling spices; ½ cup honey; 3 bay leaves and 3 basil leaves. Bring to boil and boil for 10 minutes. Pour mixture over chicken claws in jars and seal. Ready in 2 weeks.

Cranberry Relish

Helen Manning, Gay Head

Have 4 cups of cranberries and 4 cups of oranges. Wash the oranges and cranberries. Quarter the oranges so you can remove the seeds. Put the fruit through a grinder (either coarse or medium) and mix together.

BIBLIOGRAPHY

Allen, Joseph Chase. *Tales and Trails of Martha's Vineyard.* Little, Brown & Co., Boston, 1949. Published by Dukes County Historical Society.

Banks. *History of Martha's Vineyard.* Dukes County Historical Society, Edgartown, 1966.

Britton, Nathaniel and Brown, Hon., Addison. *An Illustrated Flora of the Northern United States and Canada.* Vol. I, II, III. Dover Publications, Inc., New York, 1970.

Coon, Nelson. *Using Wayside Plants.* Heathside Press, Inc., New York, 1969.

Coon, Nelson. *Wild Flowers of Martha's Vineyard.* Nelson Coon, Vineyard Haven, Mass. 1969.

Culpeper, Nicholas. *Culpeper's Complete Herbal.* W. Foulsham & Co., Ltd., London, n.d.

Gibbons, Euell. *Stalking the Blue-Eyed Scallop.* David McKay Company, Inc., New York, 1964.

Gibbons, Euell. *Stalking the Healthful Herbs.* David McKay Company, Inc., New York, 1971.

Gibbons, Euell. *Stalking the Wild Asparagus.* David McKay Company, Inc., New York, 1970.

Fernald, Merrit Lyndon. *Gray's Manual of Botany.* D. Van Nostrand Company, New York, 1970.

Grieve, Mrs. M. *A Modern Herbal.* Vol. I, II. Dover Publications, Inc., New York, 1971.

Harris, Ben Charles. *Eat the Weeds.* Barre Publishers, Barre, Mass., 1972.

House, Homer D. *Wild Flowers.* The Macmillan Company, New York, 1961.

Jacobs, Dorothy. *A Witch's Guide to Gardening.* Taplinger Publishing Co., Inc., New York, 1964.

Kierstead, Sallie Pease. *Natural Dyes.* Bruce Humphries, Inc., Boston, 1950.

Kloss, Jethro. *Back to Eden.* Lifeline Books, Riverside, Ca., 1972.

Krieger, Louis C. *The Mushroom Handbook.* Dover Publications, Inc., New York, 1967.

Medsger, Oliver Perry. *Edible Wild Plants.* The Macmillan Company, New York, 1969.

Meyers, Joseph E. *The Herbalist.* Clarence Meyer, U.S.A., 1971.

Peterson, R. T. and McKenny, Margret. *A Field Guide to the Wild Flowers.* Houghton Mifflin Co., Inc., Boston, 1968.

Ricketts, Harold William. *Wild Flowers of the United States, The Northeast States.* Vol. I. McGraw-Hill Book Company, New York, 1965.

Weiner, Michael A. *Earth Medicines - Earth Foods.* Collier Books, New York, 1972.

Woodward, Marcus. *Leaves from Gerard's Herbal.* Dover Publications, Inc., New York, 1969.